Job Hunting with Your PC

By John R. Franklin with Elizabeth L. Smith

alpha books

A Division of Prentice Hall Computer Publishing
11711 North College, Carmel, Indiana 46032 USA

Alpha Books, 11711 N. College Ave., Carmel, IN 46032

International Standard Book Number:1-56761-008-0

Library of Congress Catalog Card Number: 92-82748

95 94 93 92   8 7 6 5 4 3 2 1

Interpretation of the printing code: the rightmost number of the first series of numbers is the year of the book's printing; the rightmost number of the second series of numbers is the number of the book's printing. For example, a printing code of 92-1 shows that the first printing of the book occurred in 1992.

Printed in the United States of America.

Trademarks

Publisher
Marie Butler-Knight

Managing Editor
Elizabeth Keaffaber

Product Development Manager
Lisa A. Bucki

Acquisitions Editor
Susan Klopfer

Senior Production Editor
Linda Hawkins

Manuscript Editor
San Dee Phillips

Cover and Interior Illustrations
Steve Vanderbosch

Designer
Amy Peppler-Adams

Indexer
Loren Malloy
Tina Trettin

Special thanks to Avon Murphy and James P. McCarter for ensuring the technical accuracy of this book.

I dedicate this book as a tribute to Frank, Shirley, Esta, and the inspiring memory of Walter, for their faith, love, and understanding have brought me this far.

John Franklin, writer and engineer, labors to get the right information to the right people, at the right time. He also enjoys setting sail on crisp, spring mornings.

Steve Vanderbosch, artist, doesn't have any pets and really likes to go on vacation—especially with his wife. He also likes to snow ski, bike ride, and swim.

Contents

Introduction

If you're looking through this book or have just purchased this book, chances are you're looking for a new job. You most likely have an asset that can help you find this new job—your personal computer, or PC.

How can you use your PC to find a job? You may be surprised! In general, you can always use your PC's word processor capabilities—first, by simply putting down on paper a realistic assessment of your skills and experience.

You can use your PC to prepare your job search goals, to see (on paper!) *what it is* that you want—and *when* you want it! With word processing, or with even more specialized software, you can make tremendous progress. With a PC, you can:

- Use special application software to help discover your priorities and to set goals and objectives.

- Use special planning software to build a step-by-step strategic plan.

- Use a database to track potential employers and jobs.

- Use a word processor to create professional-looking resumes, letters, and other written documents.

- Use special application software designed to help you build a good-looking resume.

- Use a spreadsheet to keep financial records of your job search costs.

- Go on-line with telecommunications software and a modem to conduct a regional (or perhaps a world-wide) search.

With a PC as your resource, going on-line is where the job hunt of the 90s begins for many disciplines, such as engineering, data processing, business management, teaching, consulting, writing, and countless other professions. You can use your PC, modem, and special software to tap into the very best of today's marketplace—the hidden job market.

Human resource experts agree that only 3% of job opportunities are found through newspaper ads, and if you've ever tried to send your resume to a blind box ad through the employment section, you already know the frustration it can bring. With the aid of this book, you can find where many of the best opportunities are, and where they are likely to be in the future. You'll also be better prepared before you come face-to-face with the hiring authority. Why? Because there's a lot of job-related information out there—information that can put you head and shoulders above the competition, in addition to simply showing you who has a job that needs to be filled!

Using your PC to find a job is the chief focus of this book. Every area of the job search in which you can possibly use a PC will be discussed. You'll be given information on available application software, and, in some instances, you'll be shown specific features of many of the better products you can use in your job quest.

In *Job Hunting with Your PC*, you'll also receive some basic—yet critical—job hunting tips from a Human Resources Specialist. For instance, you'll be given specifics on choosing the right type of resume for your search, along with tips on how to write follow-up letters that will get the necessary attention.

System Requirements

Here's what you'll need, minimally, in computer hardware to put the ideas in this book to work for you today:

- A personal computer with at least 512K of memory and two floppy drives (or better yet, a hard disk).
- A dot-matrix, inkjet, or laser printer, and cable.
- A modem (external, or preferably, an internal).
- Telecommunications software (Procomm, and so on).
- An available phone line for the modem.

Though all of the software presented in this book supports dot-matrix, inkjet, and laser printers, it's important that you use the very best output quality available. After all, this may be your only opportunity to make a good, first impression! If you don't have ready access to a high-quality laser printer, call a quick-printer or copy shop. They can usually take your document files from disk to typeset quality print, while you wait—at a cost of a few dollars.

If you're shopping for a new printer, take a look at the inkjet types from Hewlett Packard, Cannon, and Kodak. They can produce a laser-quality resume and cover letter, at about half the initial cost of an equivalent laser printer. They also require little or no maintenance—providing you with top-quality documents for many years. Visit your local computer store for a side-by-side print comparison—you'll be impressed.

If you must print your documents on a dot-matrix printer, you can actually improve the output quality (and burn up a lot of ribbons) by using a printer enhancement program. For more information about this type of software, see Chapter 7.

Various software packages will be introduced in the appropriate chapters. These packages will include word processors, databases, spreadsheets, integrated software packages, special applications for tasks such as writing resumes and planning, and on-line software for data communications.

If some of these terms, such as word processing, modem, spreadsheets, and database are new to you, don't worry. All technical words and concepts will be defined as they are presented in the coming chapters.

If you are already comfortable with using computers and a few various software programs, you will be able to apply the concepts and principles found in this book, and will be off and running in a relatively short period of time.

Ready to begin? Let's get started!

Acknowledgments

I'd like to thank the staff at Alpha Books for their insight and determination—especially my acquisitions and development editor, Susan Klopfer, for her patient guidance, and editors San Dee Phillips and Linda Hawkins for their attention to detail.

Thanks also go to my collaborator, Elizabeth Smith, who labored to keep "human" in human resources.

Special thanks go to Leslie, my faithful partner in this endeavor and throughout my love-enriched life, for her kindness guides me through the stormy seas of life.

In Search of a Good Database

When you have the right tools, it's always easier to approach a difficult task. In this chapter, you'll learn how database software can help you organize all those crumpled lists of names, addresses of hard-to-find places, interview times, and odd characteristics of the people whom you need to impress.

If you're new to the computer world, or if you've been using a computer at work or at home and are just unfamiliar with a database, don't be alarmed. In everyday terms, a computer database is a collection of information stored in a computer, that can be used for more than one purpose. You can view the same names, addresses, and so on, in a number of different ways, depending on how and when you want it. Once these names and addresses are inserted into your database, your database and word processor can then work together to automatically insert vital information into a professional-looking letter that is very impressive. For now, think of a database as a huge file cabinet that's capable of storing a large amount of information. Your records are kept in the file drawers!

What Can a Database Do for Your Job Hunt?

If you're new to databases, you're in for a pleasant surprise! A database can help you organize and keep valuable contact lists and phone numbers, and can make writing form letters easy. Once you set up your database, you will wonder how you ever conducted a job search without it. Here is a short list of things that you can do with your database:

- Organize and keep valuable contact lists and phone numbers.

- Automatically address cover letters.

- Log and compare benefits for the jobs you're offered.

- Maintain a comprehensive job search plan.

Exploring Database Programs

There are several good database programs available—from very simple to sophisticated. For your job search, however, you may want to choose one that is relatively easy to operate, so you will be up and running quickly for your job hunt. A few of the more powerful database programs will also be listed, along with their complex features.

If you don't already have a database program, here are a few products that can ease your job hunt—especially if you're using a PC with limited disk space. Each product is placed in a price range (low to high) as follows:

Low equals under $150

Moderate equals $150 to $350

High equals over $350

- **MyDatabase, by MySoftware**   MyDatabase is a program that can be run on a single floppy disk drive computer, and can easily be customized for your specific job search needs. In addition, it can also be exported (read) by many of the more popular word processors such as Word Perfect or Microsoft Word. It can also create a pocket size list of names and addresses—very handy to carry with you during your job hunting endeavors. Price Range: Low.

  Figure 1.1 is an example of a simple database screen from the MyDatabase program. Notice that the screen format looks like a format you'd use if you were writing on index cards.

  With this software, making changes in your database is easy—you simply delete the old information and replace it with the new information. You'll never want to go back to using an old-fashioned address book again!

- **Address Book Plus, by PowerUp Software**   This program is available for both DOS-based personal computers and MacIntosh computers. Like MyDatabase, Address Book Plus will operate on a single floppy drive computer and can export information to many word processing programs. A nice feature found on this program is its ability to create lists that slip into day planners in addition to generating 8 1/2" x 11" printouts. Price Range: Low.

Figure 1.1

A simple database screen using MyDatabase software.

```
═══════════════════ File: JOBHUNT ═══════════════1═
#1      Created 07/26/92
Date 8/5/92
Company Name ABC Motors
Address 1 345 Lead Ave
Address 2 Suite 121
City Oak Hill       State OH Zip Code 56190
Telephone 313/555-6904        Fax Number 313/555-8900
Mr/Mrs/Ms MrFirst Joseph    Last White
Title Comptroller           Phone/Ext 239
Position Open  Cost Accountant
Other Personnel Ed Wright

Follow Up 8/16/92
Comments Will hire next week
```

One field

A whole record

- **Rolodex Plus, by Avery Software**   This program can be run off of a floppy or hard drive, and is capable of creating an address book that can be inserted into a Rolodex Datebook Organizer. It is available for DOS-based personal computers. Price Range: Low.

- **Microsoft Works, by Microsoft Corporation**   The database portion of this integrated package can be run from a single floppy disk drive, but it is a little easier to navigate if you have a hard drive. It can create listings that can be merged with its own word processor, and is available for DOS-based and MacIntosh computers. Price Range: Low.

- **Eight In One, by Spinnaker Software**   Eight In One operates much like Microsoft Works in that its database will create listings that will merge easily into its word processor for a great looking printout. It will operate on a single floppy or a hard drive and is available only for DOS-based computers. Price Range: Low.

Some of the more powerful and sophisticated database programs which require a hard drive and/or Windows are listed below.

- **dBASE 5.0, by Borland**   dBASE needs a hard drive and plenty of memory and is designed for use by someone who has some programming background. It's compatible with various programs, and many programs have special import capabilities to read dBASE files. dBASE has long been one of the database standards of the industry. Price Range: High.

- **Foxbase, by Microsoft**   Foxbase is a relational database designed for the MacIntosh and PC. In searches, relational databases let you match information from a field in one table with information in a corresponding field of another table. Like dBASE, it too requires a hard drive, plenty of memory, and some knowledge of programming. Price Range: High.

- **Paradox, by Borland** (Figure 1.2) Paradox is a relational database for the PC. It was developed to be user-friendly, and it is—as long as you're not doing anything too complicated. Price Range: High.

Figure 1.2

Creating a job-hunting database with Paradox.

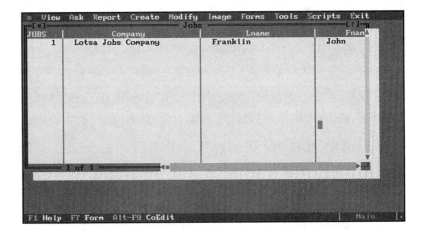

- **Windows Cardfile Utility, by Microsoft** Windows has many interesting and useful utilities. The Cardfile Utility (Figure 1.3) within the Windows program looks very similar to a 3 x 5 card, and does not require a great deal of database background. It comes standard when you purchase the Windows program. Price Range: Low.

- **SideKick Plus, by Borland** SideKick Plus is a desktop management program for the PC which includes (among other things) a calendar, notebook, and scheduler. One of the nice features of SideKick Plus is that it will run "in the background," which means that you can operate another program (a word processor, for example) and, with a few keystrokes, look at your SideKick Plus screen without backing out of your original document. Price Range: Low.

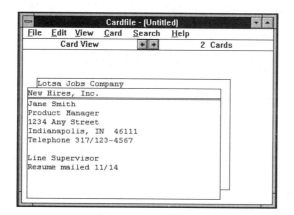

Figure 1.3

Tracking your contacts in Cardfile.

Learning Some Easy Database Words

Even if you're relatively comfortable with using computers, some of the database terminology might be new to you. Keep in mind that once you know just a few simple phrases, you'll be off and running like a pro!

Fields   Categories that you use to organize your information. Examples of fields include company names, contact names, telephone numbers, and so on. The date field is indicated in Figure 1.1.

You can sort or index your information by the fields of your choice. You can also have your database bring up specific facts and figures you've entered, such as the names of all companies in a particular state.

Records   All of the fields for each potential employer make up a record. For example, you can list the XYZ Company in your Company name field. In Figure 1.1, the entire record for ABC Motors is shown.

Files   A collection of related records. You may have several files if you want to keep some information separate. You can name one file job1hunt and another job2hunt. In Figure 1.1, the filename JOBHUNT is indicated.

Determining the Scope of Your Search

Each record you have will represent a contact; therefore, the number of records you'll have in your database will depend on your own personal job hunting goals and closing ratio. (A closing ratio simply means how many offers you get out of the number of interviews you receive.) Your closing ratio will depend upon your ability, education, experience, and closing skills (asking for the job). If you're not sure how many contacts you'll need to make, perhaps the example in the formula below will help you establish your initial target. If you're currently employed and have a very limited amount of time to interview, your beginning activity may center around obtaining two interviews per week. Your goal would be calculated as follows:

MY GOAL: To get two interviews each week.

TARGET: Need 40 contacts in my database.

REASON: I want a position in the top 10% (.10) in my field.

CLOSING RATIO: 1/2, or 50% (.5).

In this example, your goal is to get a specialized position, offered only to the top 10% in your industry. You know you have what it takes, but you also realize it's a numbers game. With your busy schedule, you have time for only two interviews each week. In order to play the odds in your favor, you'll need 40 contacts (requiring 40 records) in your database each month. This assumes that you will get one job offer for every two interviews that you receive.

FORMULA: # OF CONTACTS = (# OF INTERVIEWS divided by INDUSTRY %) * YOUR CLOSING RATIO

= (8 (2 contacts x 4 weeks) interviews / 0.10) * .50

= 40 contacts (database records)

Mating Your Database and Word Processor

When you select your database, keep in mind that you'll want to merge (or join) your files with a good word processor to create form letters and follow-up correspondence.

Your word processor will merge a database file with a document, if the database is in one of three common formats: comma delimited textfile, double quotes and comma delimited textfile, and tab delimited textfile. For a better understanding of how these data files are organized, take a look at the examples of these three types of files.

- Comma Delimited Textfile

  name,address,phone,title

- Double Quotes & Comma Delimited Textfile

  "name","address","phone","title"

- Tab Delimited Textfile

  name   address   phone   title

Most word processing programs that produce form letters are capable of merging databases in one or all of these popular formats. You shouldn't have any problem finding one that works for you.

The next two chapters will help you get your database and word processor "on speaking terms." In Chapter 2, I'll list a few of the most widely used word processors—programs that work very well with the databases we've been exploring in this chapter. In Chapter 3, you'll learn how integrated programs, software that combines the database with a word processor and spreadsheet, may be just what you need to manage your job hunt.

Word Processors: Look for Simple—Yet Stylish

First, get your foot in the door! Important business decisions, such as who will be chosen for a job interview, are often made quickly. Just getting an appointment with the right person may hinge on the quality of your written communication. In this chapter, you'll see how a word processor can help you project a winning image!

The word processor you choose for your job search might be the same one you are using at work or at home for other purposes. If you're new to word processing, you might want to use one that your friend recommends. Whatever word processor you choose, it should include all the features that you need for a successful job search.

Keep in mind that your word processor will come in handy when preparing your resume, as well as writing interview highlights and notes about prospective employers. You can also use your word processor to create:

- Your personal skills assessment.

- Your career goal sheet.

- Your job hunting plan of action.

- Lists of special training, professional seminars, and educational courses that you've completed.

- Targeted lists of references.

- The all-important query letters, cover letters, follow-up, and thank you notes.

Lots of Choices

The word processor you choose for your job search should be easy to understand and should include the special features you need for your resumes and correspondence.

Word processors are terrifically popular in the office and at home. You may already have a favorite package. So you probably already have discovered that word processing refers to the family of software programs that enable you to write, edit, print, and save documents much easier than you can with an ordinary typewriter. If you make a mistake, you can change it right on the screen—you don't have to rip the page out and start all over again.

There are many good word processing programs on the market. Make a list of the style of resume you want to produce and the features you would like to have before selecting your word processor.(This will be covered in more detail in this chapter.)

Most retail computer stores have popular word processing programs already loaded on their demonstration computers, so you can "try it before you buy it." If you don't see exactly what you want, ask the sales associate for help; she can direct you to the right program that meets your needs and skill level.

Like databases, you can find a word processing program in almost any price range:

Low	under $150
Moderate	$150 to $350
High	over $350

Some popular word processing programs include:

- **Microsoft Word, by Microsoft Corporation**   Microsoft Word requires at least two floppy drives to operate, but really works best if you have a hard drive. It doesn't require extra memory on your computer and is compatible with many database programs. Price Range: Moderate.

- **WordPerfect, by WordPerfect Corporation**   WordPerfect can be used effectively on two floppy drives but operates best on a hard drive. It is compatible with many database programs. Price Range: Moderate.

- **PFS: Write, by Spinnaker Software**   This program operates on a hard drive system and requires no additional memory. PFS:Write is compatible with many of the more popular programs, in addition to the family of PFS products. Price Range: Low.

- **WordStar, by WordStar International**   WordStar requires a hard drive and will operate under the Windows environment. Price Range: Low.

- **Ami Pro, by Lotus Development Corporation**   This program runs under the Windows environment and works very well with the other fine products from Lotus. Price Range: Moderate.

- **Windows Write, by Microsoft Corporation**   Windows Write is included in the Windows software program. It is very easy to use and offers basic editing and formatting capabilities. You can save Write files in a plain text format to export them to other Windows applications. You can bring data from other Windows into Write. You also can link Write files to data in other Windows applications using Microsoft's OLE (Object Linking and Embedding) and DDE (Dynamic Data Exchange) file linking technology. You will need a hard drive to run Windows and Windows Write. Price Range: Low.

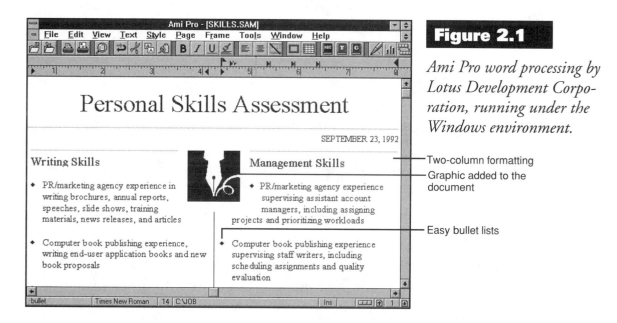

Figure 2.1

Ami Pro word processing by Lotus Development Corporation, running under the Windows environment.

Two-column formatting

Graphic added to the document

Easy bullet lists

Bells and Whistles

To produce a professional, eye-catching resume, take advantage of your word processor's special features.

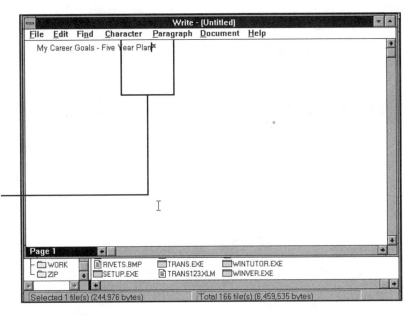

Figure 2.2

The work area of Windows Write by Microsoft Corporation.

These menus offer basic text formatting.

Fonts   Using the font capability will improve your resume. Fonts are type styles such as Courier, Times Roman, Sans Serif, and so on. When used in different sizes, fonts produce a resume that looks unique.

TIP

Stay with one font style throughout your resume, changing the font size for eye appeal and appropriateness. Most resumes are developed with a font size of 10-12 points in the body type.

Spell Checker   Most word processors include a spell check feature. If your word processor has this feature, use it, but beware of its limitations! A spell checker doesn't catch the wrong word (or the wrong form of the word). There's no substitute for reading through the resume carefully.

TIP

Reading backwards is a good way to spot mistakes. Also, have a friend check it.

Thesaurus   A thesaurus is a tool that enables you to use *precise* words when composing your resume. If your word processor has this feature, take a few moments to practice using it.

Text Enhancement   Other special features you may want your word processor to have include bold facing, underlining, italicizing, and bordering. To actually see the impact of these features on your finished document, however, you must have a printer that is supported by the software program. If you have an older printer that doesn't produce graphic characters, you may not be able to benefit from bold facing or italicizing.

If you're not sure whether you can print this special text, consult your printer manual, or call the tech-support number in your software user's guide. A call to tech-support will probably be the quickest and easiest way to get the answers you need.

TIP

Because borders can improve a resume's appearance, you might want to include this on your list of necessary word processing features.

To see what a difference the bordering feature can make in your presentation, look at the resume in Figure 2.3, and compare it with the one in Figure 2.4. See how the border provides a *frame* for your accomplishments!

The Sum Is Greater . . .

In Chapter 1, you read about merging or joining your word processor document files with your database files to create form letters and correspondence. Most popular word processors can insert the information you've stored in your database files directly into the form letter you write to be sent to your contacts.

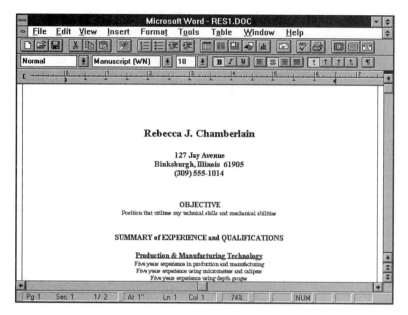

Figure 2.3

A plain resume produced using Microsoft Works by Microsoft Corporation— nothing fancy.

Your word processor takes your form letter document and scans over it—looking for the merging commands or delimiters mentioned in Chapter 1. When it locates one, it reads the field name and inserts the information from the current record into the correct field. In other words, the word processor locates the field called <<NAME>>, set off by the << >> merging commands, then inserts the proper NAME information into that field. Your word processor will follow that same process for every record in your database.

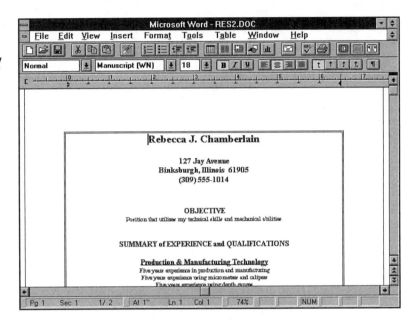

Figure 2.4

A quality resume produced using Microsoft Word by Microsoft Corporation—a border can dress up your resume.

This merging process is not difficult, if you just follow the examples in your word processor user's guide. Nearly all word processors that merge form letters provide a step-by-step tutorial to help you understand this very useful feature. Ask the sales associate in your retail computer store for more details.

If all this talk about file merging has you stressed out even before you begin your job hunt, you'll probably be better off with an integrated software program. In Chapter 3, I'll explain why an integrated program may be a better choice for you and give you several examples of the software titles available.

Powerful Stuff: Software That Does It All

In the software world, like the people world, getting along is a critical theme. Today, we have software "pieces and parts" that work together, or get along! In this chapter, you'll learn about the wonders of today's integrated software packages.

Integrated Programs?

By now, you're familiar with databases and word processors—you may even know about *spreadsheet* and *telecommunications* programs. If not, let me take a moment to briefly explain how they work.

A spreadsheet program is to numbers what a word processor is to words. Think of a spreadsheet program as a form of *electronic ledger*. You may have used this type of software in your last job to do forecasting and what-if analysis. If so, you're probably familiar with its usefulness.

A telecommunications program lets your computer *talk* to another computer—across the room or across the country. If you've ever transferred information from your computer to another computer through a telephone line, you've completed this task using telecommunications software.

Now that we have completed a brief review of these types of programs and what they do, let's look at a common problem—getting these programs to talk to one another. While many of these programs are easy to use by themselves, getting them to communicate with another program is often quite a challenge. Even though you may be familiar with a word processor program and a separate database application, tying them together so that they communicate with one another will take a little time and patience.

There's one type of program available that gives you the best of all the individual programs described above. This software is called an *integrated program*—you can have a database, a word processor, a spreadsheet, and, possibly, a telecommunications program all rolled into one seamless package. And because they are in one neat package, you don't have to worry about how to jump from one program to the next, or how you can import or export your valuable information.

What does this mean? It means that you'll have the ability to:

- Create and manage various databases.

- Produce form letters.

- Create resumes.

- Get on-line electronically to research companies and to actually apply for some jobs.

- Set goals and priorities in writing.

- Plan and track job hunting expenses.

- Keep organized and virtually conduct your entire job search while using only one software program.

Now that's power!

When you use an integrated program, you won't worry about whether your database is compatible with your word processor, or if your word processor creates documents that are compatible with your telecommunications program. You never actually leave the program. Instead, you move only from the database to the word processor to the spreadsheet—all from within the same program.

Integrated programs are usually easier to learn than individual programs. Once you master the database, you'll see that the word processor uses some of the same commands. This also is true of the telecommunications and spreadsheet programs. You're not trying to learn three or four separate programs—just three or four functions of the same program.

▼ **TIP**

What Is Compatibility? Compatibility refers to the extent to which your software parts can work in harmony on a task, without a lot of help from special hardware or software that functions as a converter. When totally different sections of integrated programs work together, like a word processor and a database, data is easily shared. Compatibility means that you can easily complete tasks like merging names and addresses with a word processing file to send out lots and lots of letters.

You'll also save a great deal of time when you use an integrated program, because the functions are all combined into one program. You never have to save your database work, exit the database program, load the word processor, open the word processor document . . . well, I think you have the general idea!

Putting It All Together

The idea of selecting an integrated program sounds complicated, but it's really quite simple.

1. Write down all of the tasks that you want to accomplish on your job hunt. These tasks should include setting goals, developing a database, creating form letters and resumes, and tracking your job hunting expenses.

2. Now write down all of the features that you want to use—special fonts, borders, and so on. When considering special fonts and borders, keep in mind that your printer must be capable of producing your documents; otherwise, you might have to use a friend's printer, or take your disk to a quick-print shop that can print your work from your diskette.

   Also remember that special fonts and borders are features found on more powerful software programs that may require a hard drive or more memory than your computer has. Always check the requirements before you install your software to make certain that it is compatible with your PC.

3. Next, take the list to your nearest retail computer store and go over your list with a knowledgeable salesperson. You can also get

help from a *computer user group*—an association of computer owners of all levels of knowledge and experience who are eager to help. Check your local public library for information about computer user groups in your area.

Most of the products available fall in the low-end price range of $150 or less. Here is a list of the more popular integrated software packages which might be recommended to you:

- **Microsoft Works, by Microsoft Corporation** Microsoft Works can operate on a floppy drive PC, but operates more easily on a hard drive PC. It is totally integrated. There is also a Windows version available for hard disk systems. Price Range: Low.

- **Eight-In-One, by Spinnaker Software** Eight-In-One can operate on a floppy drive or hard drive PC and is totally integrated. Price Range: Low.

- **PFS: First Choice, by Spinnaker Software** This application will run on a floppy drive system, and is totally integrated. Price Range: Low.

- **Microsoft Windows, by Microsoft Corporation** Windows will require a hard drive and quite a bit of memory to operate. Its operating environment has built-in integrated functions that make it easy to jump from one application to another (although it does not include spreadsheet capabilities). Price Range: Low.

- **SideKick Plus, by Borland International** SideKick Plus requires a hard drive and has a built-in phone book and scheduler. It may require quite a bit of memory. Price Range: Low.

Keep in mind that all of these programs are easy to use, and they all provide help screens to assist you every step of the way. Some even have a tutorial so that you can learn the program quickly and easily while you're actually using it. That's much more fun than just reading the manual, though some programs provide good, easy-to-read documentation.

Need more help? Stroll through a bookstore where you will find shelves overflowing with many friendly computer books, such as *The First Book of Microsoft Works,* by Debbie Walkowski, or *The First Book of Microsoft Works for Windows,* by Clayton Walnum.

Tying Your Features Together

If you decide to use an integrated software program, you can achieve tremendous results in your job search in a very short period of time. Here's how you can tie it all together:

1. Fill in your database with dates, contact names, titles of key personnel, positions available, and so on (see Figure 3.1).

2. Go to your word processor and compose a form letter (see Figure 3.2) that has *merge fields*—the fields you created to accept the appropriate information from your database. For example, if you're using Microsoft Works, you simply type in the name of the field, followed by a colon (:). This tells the word processor that information from a database file will be merged into this field.

   Next the word processor will ask you how long the field should be. You respond with an adequate number of characters for that field, then move on to the next merge field. Do this for each field—merging names, addresses, and so on.

3. Now merge (or join) the information in your database to fill in the headings, salutations, job openings, and so on. (For detailed information on how to make form letters from your database, see Chapter 10.)

Figure 3.1

A database record, ready to link to a form letter.

```
┌─────────────────────────── DB2.WDB ───────────────────────────┐
│ DATE: 7/20/92                                                  │
│ COMPANY NAME: Chamberlain Press, Inc.                          │
│ ADDRESS 1: 100 Main St                                         │
│ ADDRESS 2: P O Box 16                                          │
│ CITY: Muscatine              STATE: IA  ZIP CODE:      30940   │
│                                                                │
│ CONTACT                      MR/MRS/MS: Mr.                    │
│ FIRST NAME: Walter           LAST NAME: Chamberlain            │
│ TITLE: President             PHONE NUMBER: 403/555-1217        │
│ FAX NUMBER: 403/555-7754                                       │
│                                                                │
│ OTHER PERSONNEL: Esta Kelly, Operations Mgr                    │
│ POSITION OPEN:                                                 │
│ FOLLOW UP DATE:              9/1/92                            │
│                                                                │
│ COMMENTS: Expanding Plant & Personnel in October, 1992        │
└────────────────────────────────────────────────────────────────┘
```

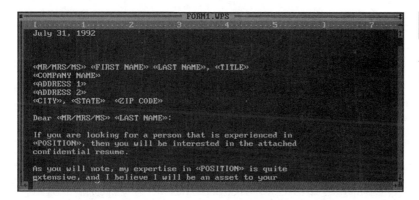

Figure 3.2

A typical form letter, ready to pull in a database.

4. Next create a job search budget and expense report using the spreadsheet capabilities. Your spreadsheet may look like the example in Figure 3.3.

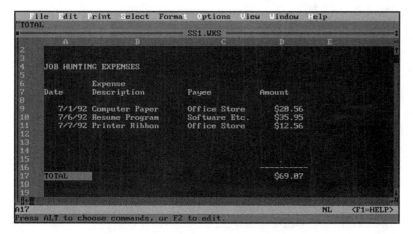

Figure 3.3

Sample expense tracking spreadsheet.

Some of the expenses you will want to track while conducting your job search are:

- Paper costs

- Gasoline and travel expense

- Office supply expenses

- Printing costs

It's a good idea to be specific and to break down your expenses into as many categories as you possibly can. Doing this will allow you to create a more realistic budget figure, and will also let you know exactly where you are financially on your job search.

Keeping accurate records on your spreadsheet now will save you money and frustration at tax time.

- You'll now be able to keep track of the entire job hunt in one location.

- You'll be working more efficiently. (Many people like to sit in front of their computers while making follow-up telephone calls so they can update their file information quickly.)

In Chapter 10, I'll show you what your finished documents will look like. You'll be amazed at how quickly you can create and maintain files like the ones in these examples. You'll also be pleased with the final results—your professional and personalized cover letters.

Though integrated programs are a very productive tool to use for your job hunt—and in your workplace after you get that new job— you may also want to consider using a resume program. This is a relatively new type of program, but there are already several good ones available. In Chapter 4, I'll explain what a resume program is and what it can do to help you better manage your job hunt.

No Time to Relax: Using Specialized Resume Software

Remember The Graduate, *when a young college senior gets advice from an executive on the merits of specialization? Well, even if you don't remember this 60s movie, the executive's advice wasn't too bad. You'll learn about today's benefit of specialization as you read this chapter on tracking down software that specializes in making you look great.*

Producing A Professional-looking Resume

Most resume programs are actually integrated database and word processing programs designed especially for you, the job hunter. They're packed full of nice features and helpful hints to help you focus your efforts and to make your job search successful.

You'll find that not only does a resume program produce a professional looking document with its extra font capabilities, but some are equipped with a built-in database program to help you file contact lists, names, addresses, phone numbers, and so on. Some of the better resume programs, like *PFS:Resume & Job Search Pro* (in Figures 4.1 and 4.2), even have personal schedulers and follow-up calendars to remind you of appointments and interviews.

Figure 4.1

Database features of PFS:Resume & Job Search Pro.

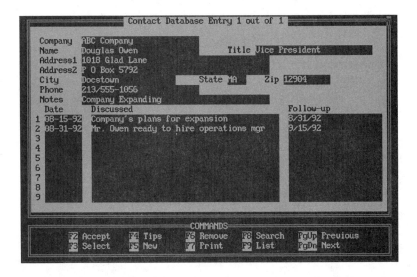

If you're unclear on what position or line of work you want to enter, again, look to the more advanced resume programs. They can help you evaluate your skills, your education, your experience levels, and so on.

TIP

You may want your resume program to include a question-and-answer session to sharpen your interview skills. This feature, along with the list of sample interview questions in Appendix A, can go a long way in getting you ready for the interview.

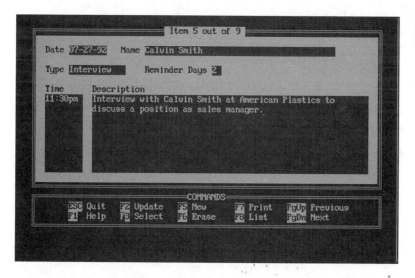

Figure 4.2

Using specialized software to track your interviews.

Some of the simpler resume packages are designed to work in conjunction with your word processor and include templates to use to fill in your background and personal information.

A few resume programs (all priced under $150) you might consider are:

- **PFS:Resume & Job Search Pro, by Spinnaker Software PFS**: Resume & Job Search Pro is a sophisticated, yet easy-to-use program that not only combines resume formats, but will help you track your contacts and keep organized. Its features include: a built-in word processor for writing cover letters and correspondence, a spell checker & thesaurus, an envelope writing feature, a contact/employer database, and a reminder system and built-in calendar for appointment scheduling.

  This software also contains on-line help screens to help you on any screen. A manual is also included that will give you tips on job negotiating, interviewing techniques and the proper way to write cover letters. The program also has easy-to-use templates for a variety of careers that can easily be altered to suit your needs. PFS:Resume & Job Search Pro works best with a hard drive.

- **Expert Resume, by Expert Software**   Expert Resume is a very easy-to-use program and includes sample resume designs that can be customized. This program also includes a spell checker and supports either a dual floppy PC or a hard drive PC. It is also capable of supporting standard dot matrix printers or laser printers. You will need DOS 2.0 or higher to operate Expert Resume.

- **Key Resume Writer, by Softkey Software Products, Inc.**   Key Resume Writer is a program that requires the use of your word processor to operate, but works well with many word processors. A few of the more popular word processing programs that Key will operate with include Microsoft Word, WordPerfect, WordStar, Harmony, Displaywrite 4, and Office Writer. Key Resume Writer provides more than 130 resumes, cover letters, and phrases. Letters are organized into categories for easy access. You can also merge a selected resume with the name and address information stored in your Address Cardfile.

  Included in the software package is your personal copy of "Resumes That Knock 'Em Dead" by Martin John Yate. In order to operate Key Resume Writer, you will need a PC with DOS 2.1 or higher and a hard drive.

To find the resume program that's right for you, you may want to purchase a personal computer magazine or even search through back issues of magazines at your local public library. Most publications have software reviews or list specific features about a software program. There are many excellent resume packages available, and, chances are, there's one on the market that will be just right for you.

Extra Features Help

Whatever resume program you choose, you'll want to make sure it has all of the basic features. The program you choose should have enough flexibility to let you easily tailor its templates (or forms) to suit your education and experience level. Remember, you must feel comfortable with the end product—your resume—so you can send it with pride. Here's a handy shopping list that might help you in deciding on the package that's just right for you:

- **Resume Templates**   Although you may have in mind what resume you want to use for your specific career path, it is always handy to create a resume from templates—make sure, however, that the program you choose will have an option to alter it to suit your needs.

- **Spell Checker/Thesaurus**   These things are a must when shopping for a good resume program. A spell checker is extremely handy as a safeguard for your document.

TIP

Keep in mind that even though a word is spelled correctly, it may be incorrect in your sentence structure. A good habit to get into is to read your finished document backwards to pick up on words like "you" and "your". A thesaurus saves so much time and effort, you will not want to be without one in your program. It will help you to select just the right action words to pack a punch in your resume.

- **Contact Lists and Database**   If you do not have a database, you might consider purchasing a resume program that will include your valuable contact lists and database functions. Be sure that it will be flexible enough that you can change or add some fields. You might want to consider a program that will do mailing lists from your contact database as a bonus feature.

- **Word Processing Capabilities**   If you do not plan to use a separate word processor, then you may want to consider a resume program with built-in word processing capabilities. If you already have a word processor, then you may want to choose a "template" program that works with your word processor. If you are going to use a template program, make certain that it is compatible with your word processor. (Many template programs will have a list of compatible software packages on the back of the box.)

- **Calendars and Appointment Schedulers**   Although this is not a must, it is certainly a nice feature to look for when shopping for a resume program. Calendars and appointment schedulers will keep you on top of your search, reminding you of valuable interviews and appointments. This feature can not only be used in your job search, but you may find it helpful to organize your personal and family schedules as well. See Figure 4.3 for a sample appointment reminder feature.

- **On-Line Help**   It's always a good idea to look for a program with on-line help. In case you are not familiar with this, on-line help is an instruction manual that can be accessed on your screen with a touch of a button, and usually without leaving the task you are in. It can be a tremendous help if you are new to a program, but need to get started quickly in producing your resume.

- **Hard/Floppy Drive Systems**   Before you purchase any program, always make sure that it can operate on your system. If you do not have a hard drive, you need to purchase a program that will work on a single floppy or dual floppy drive system.

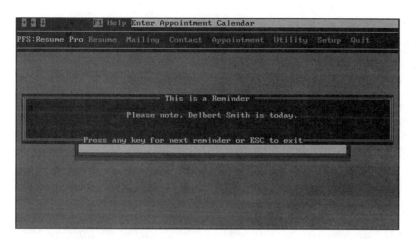

Figure 4.3

An appointment reminder—found in many popular resume software packages.

- **Operating System Compatibility**   Before you leave home on your search for a good resume program, it's a good idea to jot down all that you know about your computer—what version of DOS do you have? Is your monitor monochrome (just one color) or color—is it EGA, VGA, etc.? Do you have a hard drive? What size is your disk drive—3 1/2 or 5 1/4? Write down everything you know about your computer before you purchase your package. Once you have that list you can be better prepared in making your software decisions.

- **Printer Compatibility**   Make note of your printer and its capabilities. Most programs will list the printers that they are compatible with right on the package.

TIP

When software shopping, you'll find that less expensive resume applications often include only a small number of templates. They're usually harder to customize, too. Also, notice that resume software varies in how templates are tailored.

If your resume program will be the only software you'll be using on your job search, be sure it includes a database to store those valuable contact lists and telephone numbers like the *PFS:Resume & Job Search Pro* example in Figure 4.2.

Using a thesaurus can be a great help when composing your resume. Before you purchase a program, make sure that the one you choose has a thesaurus geared toward job-hunting. You want your resume to stand head and shoulders above the rest, and a little investment now will go a long way in landing that successful position. See Figure 4.4 for a sample thesaurus screen.

Spell check features are also essential—you'd be surprised at how many resumes have incorrect spelling. Some companies actually hire people to check spelling on all incoming resumes. See Figure 4.5 to see how basic spell check features work.

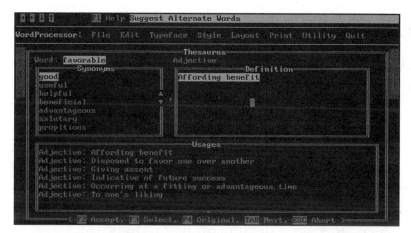

Figure 4.4

A Sample thesaurus screen found in PFS: Resume & Job Search Pro.

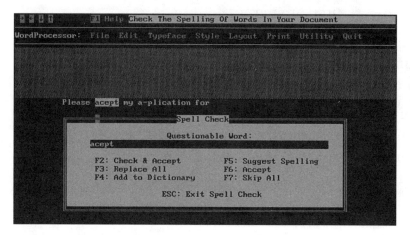

Figure 4.5

A sample spell check screen found in PFS:Resume & Job Search Pro.

Understanding the Drawbacks of Resume Software

With all that a resume program can offer, there are also some limitations that should be considered. Here are just a few examples of some of the drawbacks you may experience with the resume program you choose:

- **Limited Font Capability**   Some resume programs have limited fonts to choose from. Even though there are font packages on the market that will enhance your document, not all font packages will import into a resume program.

- **Limited Graphics**   Since there are little or no graphic capabilities in most resume programs, you will probably not be able to produce special effects—like borders and lines.

- **Format Limitations**   Some programs will allow you to alter the style, or format their resume template only slightly. You may have to give up some style for the sake of price—the more sophisticated programs will allow you to change the style, but they cost a little more.

Other limitations might include a limit to the number and the type of fields you'll be merging from within the database. Lastly, you'll probably have to give up some special effects like the border, because most resume programs only produce traditional-styled documents—without graphics, such as borders and lines.

Getting It Together: Special Productivity Tools

Have you ever known someone who was really, really messy? You know this person—coffee cups resting on computer printouts; stacks and piles of stuff everywhere in sight (and important papers stuffed out of sight, way back in small drawers). In this chapter, you'll read about getting your act together and keeping it together with some special PC tools. Now find this friend quick and tell him or her about this book!

String on Your Finger

The *personal productivity concept* is not a new one—business people have been using it for years to keep organized, to set appointments, to keep telephone listings, and so on. You may know several people who keep date book organizers on their desks or in their briefcases. These people are practicing personal productivity.

You can benefit from having your own personal productivity system on your PC—you'll have your entire job hunt organized in one place.

Electronic Reminders

Personal productivity programs will actually enhance your job search by reminding you of valuable follow-up phone calls, correspondence, luncheon appointments, and so on. For instance, if you tell a prospective employer that you will call next Tuesday at 1:30 p.m., enter that day and time in your program so that your PC will remind you to make the call.

Keeping on top of your commitments will make a great impression with any hiring authority. That's one example of how a personal productivity program can keep you on top of things. Here's a list of other benefits that this type of software has to offer:

- A to-do list that can later be prioritized and checked as tasks are completed.

- A place for recurring dates such as birthdays, holidays, and anniversaries.

- The ability to create personal and business schedules and merge the two together to avoid conflicts.

- The ability to create printouts to inform everyone, especially family members, of your schedule. This will ensure the support and assistance that you need to create a good jobhunting environment.

- A handy printout that can be used to supplement your day-planner organizer.

In a world of increasing time pressures, isn't it nice to know that the computer can help you get back a portion of your day. With the increased time pressures of holding down a job while looking for a new one, personal productivity programs can be a real asset when juggling these multiple schedules.

A Look at Your Choices

There are many productivity programs on the market today—and more on the way. Even though their basic concept is the same, most vary in what they can do.

Some programs signal you when it's time to make that phone call by beeping at you. Some use color (if you have a color monitor) to block out portions of your day with a different color to let you know how much of your schedule is already committed to tasks and appointments. In Figure 5.1, you can see how OnTime, by Campbell Services, provides both of these important features.

There are even programs that look (and print) exactly like the pages of a date book organizer. In Figure 5.2, you can see the print preview of Calendar Creator Plus, by PowerUp Software. This program produces a printed page that can be inserted in many of the popular date book organizers.

Figure 5.1

Planning your day with OnTime personal productivity software.

A scheduled appointment, with alarm set

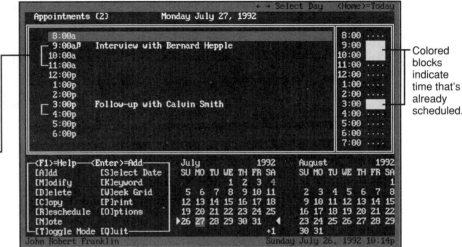

Colored blocks indicate time that's already scheduled.

Figure 5.2

You can print out pages from a computerized date book using Calendar Creator Plus.

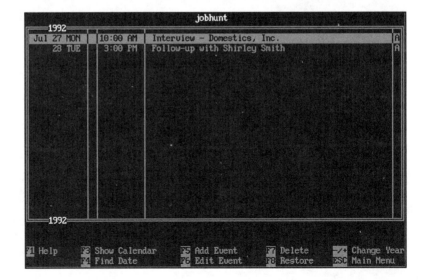

Taking Care of Tomorrow

Whatever you need to keep current with your search, there is probably a personal productivity program to meet your needs. If you're not sure what you want in a personal productivity program, once again, write down a list of the things you may want and then go shopping at your local software store.

Prices will vary depending on features, but most programs are relatively inexpensive and easy to use. Whichever software program you choose, make sure it has most of the following features:

- It should be able to run effectively on your computer. (If you don't have a hard drive, make sure your program can run on a floppy drive PC.)

- Make sure that the program you choose can generate reports on your printer.

- If you're planning to use your program to supplement your date book organizer, make sure that it will support the same size pages found in your date book.

If you intend to use your printout from your productivity program without inserting it into your date book, you might want to look at a program like OnTime, by Campbell Services. While providing all the basic and advanced features of a personal productivity program,

OnTime produces a unique threefold printout printed on both sides. The first side provides a month to six weeks of schedules at a glance. The other side provides a to-do list, a year-at-a-glance, and a list of your daily appointments.

When selecting your program, keep in mind what you'll need for the future. Not only is this a wonderful tool for your job search, but this is also a program that you can take with you to use when you start your new career. So, put some thought into the type of position you're seeking and the environment in which you'll be working.

TIP

Getting organized—and keeping organized—will certainly go a long way to impress your supervisor and maybe even put you on the fast track to a promotion.

Here are a few of the programs available for your personal productivity needs, most in the low (under $150) price range:

- **OnTime, by Campbell Services, Inc.** OnTime can run on a floppy or hard drive system, and while it does support a dot-matrix printer, its unique threefold printout is available only on a laser printer. If you don't have a laser printer, not to worry—Laser Twin by Metro Software (see Chapter 7) can make your dot-matrix printer think that it's a laser printer.

- **Calendar Creator Plus, by PowerUp Software**   Calendar Creator Plus can run on a floppy or hard drive PC and supports laser, inkjet, and dot-matrix printers. Calendar Creator Plus also provides printouts that will fit in most date book organizers.

- **Eight-In-One, by Spinnaker Software** (also listed with integrated software in Chapter 3)   Eight-In-One, which is actually an integrated program, can run on a floppy or hard drive PC and supports laser, inkjet, and dot-matrix printers.

- **Microsoft Windows Calendar, by Microsoft Corp.**   Microsoft Windows has a Calendar accessory that enables you to schedule appointments and events. This application requires a hard drive and supports laser, inkjet, and dot-matrix printers.

- **SideKick Plus, by Borland International**   SideKick Plus has been on the market almost as long as the PC. This program requires a hard drive and supports laser, inkjet, and dot-matrix printers.

Some resume programs will also have a small personal productivity database built-in their package. Check all the features before you make your purchase. You may want to use both—your resume program now, and your personal productivity program now and when you land your job.

TIP

Many readers may find scheduling easier by using the scheduling module available on their operating system or the shell application. Microsoft Windows, SideKick Plus, and Norton Desktop for Windows, for instance, have very useful calendar features.

In Chapter 10, you'll see how your personal productivity program will pay off as you start to follow-up on job leads. Now that you know the programs available for a successful job search and understand how they can work with one another, let's get started!

Developing Your Job Search Database

You've assembled your software and hardware tools—now it really is time to get moving! In this chapter, you'll build a structure for your job search (database) to organize all of the facts and figures you'll be collecting about possible employers.

Planning Your Database

The preliminaries are over—you've pulled together the software and hardware you'll be using for your job hunt. It's time to put these tools to work; beginning with your employment database is a logical first step.

In order to build your employment database, you need to pull information from as many employment services and sources as possible. Where will this information come from, you may ask? Here are just a few of the sources you can use in putting together your employment database:

- **Trade publications and magazines**   If you belong to a profes-sional organization or association, chances are you receive publica-tions on a quarterly or monthly basis. These publications are rich in opportunities in one of two ways. First, they will often list jobs available. Second, they will tell you of growth companies and industries that you can use to build your contact list.

- **Company fliers and brochures**   Company fliers and brochures tell you more specific information about job opportunities. Often they include opportunities, such as the trade publications, with one exception—they list names of key people within a company. This is what sets company fliers and brochures apart from trade publications and magazines. Fliers and brochures can provide you with a wealth of information.

- **Business section of the weekly newspapers**   The business section can give you a pretty accurate overview of how a company is doing—and will also give you information on how a company is growing and what opportunities might be available.

- **Contacts with the competition**   Often a company will be aware of business transactions and growth patterns of their competitors. They may have information on a competing company before it goes public.

If you see that a company is expanding its work force, think for a moment if that expansion might lead to a position for which you are qualified. This is a great way to get a jump on your competition. If you respond before they have a chance to advertise in the newspaper employment ads, you have increased your chances immeasurably.

- **Company employees** The people that you know and live near work somewhere, and if you let them know very early of your efforts to find a job, chances are they will keep an eye and ear open at their place of employment that will match your qualifications.

- **Word of mouth** You can never communicate too much with other people during your job search. Ask other people about what they think about a particular company or companies. You will find that people are very willing to share what they know about a company's background, and they will probably recommend a few more companies that you may want to contact.

- **Notes following interviews** Listen closely in an interview situation. Even if it doesn't feel as if this is the right job for you, listen to what the interviewer has to say—they may know about other companies that are looking for a good, qualified person.

Collect Facts Daily

Now that you know where to collect that information, make it a practice to collect information on a daily basis, and enter that information on your database. You want to constantly be updating and reviewing your job search data. So, it is time to turn your attention to the development of the database structure.

With any database, you must first develop a structure, naming fields or categories to hold all of the critical data (facts and figures) about potential employers. For instance, you'll want to track the company name, address, city, state, and zip code. You'll also want to keep track of the names of key people, their titles, and so on. You'll organize this data into separate records stored in your electronic job search files.

Setting up your database is one of the most vital steps you'll take to ensure a successful job hunt, so be prepared to invest a great amount of time. It is best to get into a daily habit of reviewing and entering information into your database. In addition to that, plan to spend three to four hours setting up your database initially, and an hour each weekend to organize and make sure you have current information. It is important to remember that cautious preparation now can save you countless hours of time and frustration later.

Developing Fields

Once you've selected and installed your database software, you can begin developing your database by typing in field names. *Fields*, as discussed in Chapter 1, are categories that you'll use later to sort your information.

When you choose data fields within your stand-alone or integrated software program, get as detailed as possible—breaking down titles, company divisions, and so on into individual data fields.

For instance, you'll want to have separate field names such as "Mr./ Mrs./Ms." and "Title" to include the person's position with the company. Figure 6.1 shows how these individual data fields would appear within your database file, using Microsoft Works. The more specific you get now in creating your fields, the easier it will be later when you create form letters and correspondence.

If you've decided to collect your employer contact information with specialized software such as PFS's Resume & Job Search Pro, instead of traditional database software, you'll probably find that specific fields are already set up for your use.

Using a contact file built into special software can be a real time-saving device. Just be sure to check the program features closely before you make your purchase. Make sure that the database—which is a part of the program—includes all of the features you need. For example, does the database have memo fields? Are you limited to a small number of fields? Can you easily sort or index the database? You may or may not need these features. It is better to decide what you need, however, before you make a purchase and find that you can't live with the limitations.

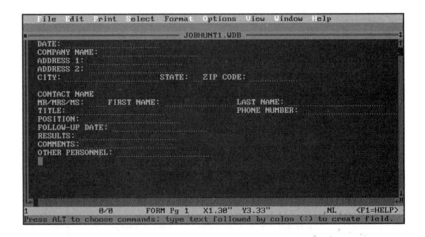

Figure 6.1

A simple database screen using Microsoft Works.

> **TIP**
>
> *Some nondatabase software programs won't let you alter their contact lists. Choose the program that has the most flexibility—remember, this is your job search and you'll want to be able to keep track of any and all information you need.*

Including Important Information

Here are some basic categories that you can use as fields in your database. (In Chapter 10, you'll see how to include even more fields to enhance your job search.)

- **Date**

    Always include an initial date—this lets you know how current your information is. For many database programs, you'll need to enter dates in mm/dd/yy format.

    Name this field I_DATE.

    Specify it as a date field.

    Give it about eight spaces.

By specifying I_DATE as a date field, most database software, such as Microsoft Works, lets you sort your records by the *date* field. This will be a great help later, as you begin to organize and maintain the contacts in your database. You'll be able to see how long you've been working with a certain contact person to evaluate whether you should continue working with that contact or spend more time working with newer contacts.

Most database software has a special date format. Date fields allow special sorting possibilities, such as sorting all of your records by certain months.

- **Company Name**

  Make sure when you fill in your records that this is the complete and accurate spelling of the company name—nothing ruins correspondence more than having the company name incorrect or incomplete. Later on, you may want to set up another field and label it "division" or "department" (see Chapter 10 for more details).

  Name this field CO_NAME.

  Assign it alphanumeric status.

  Give it about 25 spaces.

Carefully consider the number of characters for each field. This makes data entry and viewing records easier.

- **Company Address Line 1**

  This will be used for the street address. Always use the complete address when mailing your resumes and letters.

  Name this field CO_ADR1.

  Specify it as alphanumeric.

  Give it about 25 spaces.

- **Company Address Line 2**

  You'll use this address line for a post office box, suite number, or floor number—include all the information you can in this field to ensure that your correspondence will be addressed correctly.

  Name this field CO_ADR2.

  Designate it alphanumeric.

  Assign it about 25 spaces.

- **City**

  Include sufficient space in this field—about 30 to 35 spaces should do. You can always expand this field later, but allow plenty of room now. This field is, of course, where the city name goes!

  Give this field a recognizable name, like CITY.

  Categorize it as alphanumeric.

  Assign about 35 spaces.

- **State**

  Two spaces for this field is sufficient since virtually all businesses use the standard two letter abbreviation for state names. If you don't know what the accepted abbreviations are for out-of-state correspondence, contact your local post office.

  Make this field name easy—STATE.

  Indicate it as alphanumeric.

  Give it two spaces.

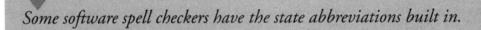

Some software spell checkers have the state abbreviations built in.

- **Zip Code**

  You need space for the five digit code, a space for a dash and four spaces for the zip sort number now used. You may not use all ten spaces on most records, but it is handy to have when you need to have the standard nine digit zip code. Keep life simple and

  Give this field a name such as ZIP.

  Designate it as alphanumeric with 10 spaces.

- **Company Telephone Number**

  Allow enough room for the area code and full phone number. Some resume programs have a special field format just for phone numbers. If yours does, take advantage of it—it'll probably separate the area code and the number for you automatically.

  Give this field a name like CO_PHONE.

  Designate it alphanumeric.

  Allow for about 15 spaces.

- **Mr/Mrs/Ms**

  Setting up a separate field for this now will save time and frustration when you send your correspondence later. You'll also use this field if you have to address someone with a doctorate degree, for instance, Dr. Frank Jones. Since you want to make a great first impression, always make certain you enter the title correctly.

  Name this field STATUS.

  Indicate that it's alphanumeric.

  Give it about five spaces.

- **Contact First Name**

  Always type the correct spelling, and use the long version of the person's first name in your written communication, unless you are specifically instructed to use the short version. For instance, you'll want to use the name Elizabeth, instead of Beth.

  Name this field CONT_FN.

  Designate it alphanumeric.

  Give it 25 spaces, or so.

- **Contact Last Name**

  Again, make certain you spell the last name correctly—if your resume looks great and you are qualified for a job, but you've misspelled the contact's last name, you may not be considered for the position.

  Call this field CON_LN.

  Designate it as alphanumeric.

  Allow about 30–35 spaces for your record because some last names are quite lengthy.

- **Contact Title**

  This will be used for records such as Vice President, Human Resources Director, and so on.

Name this field CON_TTL.

Indicate it as alphanumeric.

Give it about 25 spaces.

- **Contact Telephone**

  You'll use this field for extension numbers or full direct phone numbers. You may not have this number when you fill in the initial information, but you may want to fill it in, once you get further along in your job search.

  Name this field CON_TEL.

  Designate it alphanumeric.

  Give it about 15 spaces.

- **Position**

  You'll use this to track positions open or desired. In Chapter 10, you'll see how this field can come in handy when you produce initial correspondence and follow-up letters.

  Define this field as alphanumeric.

  Give it about 15 spaces.

  Call it POS.

- **Follow-Up Date**

  Use this as a reminder to follow up with phone calls or letters. This field is vital if you want to keep organized, ensuring a successful job search. Although you may be using a project management or time management program, keep this field in your database. It will be much easier to create your follow-up tasks.

  Give this field a name such as F_U_D.

  Specify it as a date field.

- **Results**

  Use this field for the results of your job hunting efforts. You may want to use your own personal ranking system based on a number scale, or you may jot down what your results were. For instance, you may want to provide information like "good," "excellent," and so on.

  Name this field RESULTS.

  Designate it as alphanumeric.

  Give it about 25 spaces, or so.

- **Comments**

  This lets you add any information you find about the company. For instance, you may find that the company will be expanding in a few months, so you may want to track that in your comments section. The comments section will also come in handy for recording information you learn through your *grapevine* of contacts.

Name this field COMMENT.

Designate it as a memo field.

These are the *basic* information fields you'll want to use in your job hunting database, however, you may want to add fields such as "Other Personnel" for support people in the office. You may even want to include four or five more fields for a secondary contact, such as human resource directors, and so on.

Adding these specific fields can pay off when you sort your database to get a little better insight and information on your contact list as a whole. For example, let's say that you wanted to sort all your data to find all the positions available in the Midwest. You simply use your sort function on your database and ask the program to find all the records from a region (if you want to set up a field that way) or states. When you break down information into many specific pieces, your database becomes very manageable, and you will find that you can retrieve your records so much easier.

In Chapter 10, you'll learn how to add more specific information to your database and how to create your own reference library.

Don't worry if you take up more than one page of data on your screen. Just concentrate on getting as much information as you can for a successful job search. Many databases let you use the up or down arrow keys, or page up or page down keys on your keyboard so that you can view the remaining fields in your database.

Use your database as "command central." By creating specific information, you can take pieces of data and construct an overview of prospective employers and their activities in business. You'll see how they size up against their competitors.

Chapter 8 will go into more detail on how you can find the information to put into your database about prospective employers.

Keep in mind that the more detail you put into your fields now, the better off you'll be later in your job search. After all, you can't search your database for vital information if you never created a place to store it.

Using Word Processing And Other Special Software to Build a Winning Resume

Resume building gives you time to feel good—about you. Think back to when you finished a big project on time and under cost, or when you received a volunteer award. Give yourself a pat on the back—and then turn on your PC and enter that valuable data right now!

Developing your interview-winning resume on your PC isn't as complex as you might think. With just a few steps, you'll be able to prepare a resume that can get you the interview that lands the job!

By using your word processor to create the structure of your job history, qualifications, education, and accomplishments, you can create many different versions without doing extra typing. You can do this quickly and easily with your word processor because you don't have to retype your document again and again when you use the cut and paste feature.

Build a Personal Work History

First build a personal work history. You'll find yourself doing some writing and editing, but your word processor can turn almost any big writing project into a simple task. Think of your personal worksheet as a place to list all of your past work history and accomplishments, and as a building block for producing a professional-looking resume—one that separates your qualifications from all of the other people out there looking for work, too!

By using a personal worksheet, you'll develop a resume that reflects your

- Experience

- Potential

- Accomplishments

Plan to spend some time on this task, and don't worry for now if you get items out of order. Remember, with your PC's word processor, you can always use your *cut and paste* feature later to organize the items into an order that is best for a specific job opportunity.

Your History File

Create a document labeled "history" (you may need a shorter file name on some word processors), and type in the *description headings* (see Figure 7.1).

```
                          WORK HISTORY

        Dates (to/from):
        Firm:
        Address:
        Job Title:
        Last Salary:

        Major Duties:




        Knowledge required
        to perform the work:

        Abilities required
        to do the work:

        Skills required to
        perform the work:

        Accomplishments:

        Specialized Training:
```

Figure 7.1

Typical description headings for a resume-building history file.

Begin with the dates when you started and ended your work, the name and address of the company for which you worked, your job title with a brief explanation, and your last salary level.

Next, describe your major duties—those duties that required the greater portion of your time. If possible, try to divide each duty into its required *activities*. For example, if one of your duties involved producing a monthly newsletter on your PC, your activities list might look something like this:

Major Duties: Produced monthly company newsletter

- Established guidelines for contributors.

- Established cut-off dates for submissions.

- Imported text files into desktop publisher.

By listing these newsletter activities, you can document your project management and desktop publishing experience. This information will help when you begin to customize your resume for a particular job description, and it will also help a prospective employer evaluate the skills you bring to the job.

Once you list your duties and activities information, your personal worksheet may look like Figure 7.2.

Notice that activities are listed directly below the duties they support. If you're an over-achiever and need more space to list all of your major duties and their activities, no problem. With your word processor, you can easily expand this section into an entire page-long section, if you like!

Figure 7.2

Building a personal worksheet.

```
                    WORK HISTORY

Dates (to/from):    5/88 - 8/91
Firm:               W & E ENTERPRISES
Address:            120 Main, Amerberg, PA 12056
Job Title:          Human Resource Assistant
Last Salary:        $23,500

Major Duties:       Produce monthly company newsletter
                       -Import text files into publishing program
                    Keep employee insurance records
                       -Organize files using color coding system

Knowledge required
to perform the work:        Filing systems, insurance codes, desktop
                            publishing

Abilities required
to do the work:             Organizational skills, time management

Skills required to
perform the work:           Personal Computing

Accomplishments:            Developed new color-coded filing system

Specialized Training:       Completed desktop publishing seminar in
                            December, 1991
```

Recall Duties, Activities

In the next step, describe the knowledge, abilities, and skills required to do your job. Because you took the time to list all of the activities that supported the major duties of your job, you've made this next step a lot easier.

TIP

Trying to describe previous job duties? And you're stuck? Pretend you're hiring someone for your old position, then jot down what's needed to do the work you were doing!

Now it's time to move to the accomplishments section. This part is especially important, because it proves that you can do what you say you can. Did you

- Save money for the company?

- Receive an award, or promotion?

- Lead a complex project or task?

When you list each accomplishment, focus on how it became a benefit to your employer. For example, you may have received a promotion for managing projects successfully. You can present that in the form of a *benefit* by writing: "Three years of successful project management—leading to significant cost reductions in production." When you go in for the interview, you can then mention that your project management efforts resulted in a promotion. Boast a little—you've earned it.

Training Enhances Your Resume

Your last entry should be training—either company-provided or independent. Did you attend workshops, seminars, department training, or work toward your degree? Did you learn to use new products, services, or equipment?

Now Do It All Again!

Repeat this process for all positions that you've held within the past 8–10 years. If you've held several positions within one company, treat each job independently.

TIP

If you've been out of work for several years, look carefully at your volunteer experience and make a work sheet for those activities. Show that unemployment hasn't kept you inactive and out of touch!

By the time you're finished, you may have several pages of accomplishments in your document. Make a separate document for each job you've held, but remember that using a single document is easier to handle if you want to use your word processor's *cut and paste* features.

List Your References

Include a heading for *references*, or create a separate file for them. It's a good idea to list 6 to 12 people who have known you in the work setting and will give you a good recommendation. Type in their complete names, titles, complete addresses (with zip code), and telephone numbers.

TIP

When tracking your references, you can add a note field reminding you of special relationships with each individual—availability for telephone calls, particular expertise, and so on. We don't always know how someone might be able to help us in talking with a future employer.

You'll use your references file later to produce a *reference sheet*, if your prospective employer requests one. For more information on how you should handle references, see the tips on building a reference sheet in Appendix A.

Setting Up Resume Styles: Using Word Processing, Desktop Publishing, or Special Resume Software

Your resume style reflects who you are, and what kind of position you're seeking. There are several types of resume formats that are acceptable, and they can all be easily produced on your word processor, desktop publisher, or resume software.

Don't worry if your word processor has limited capabilities to make a fancy resume—low end word processing packages simply aren't going to have the multitude of features you'll find in higher priced software.

Often you can take your disk file to a copy shop or desktop publisher, and they can make a professional looking resume for you. These and other resume services are listed in the yellow pages under desktop publishing services, quick copy shops, or copy service bureaus.

Luisa Burns, president of one such service bureau located in Indianapolis, IN, recommends that two heads are often better than one, when sprucing up a resume. "When we're working to make a document look better, we ask our client what they want to accomplish; then we help them meet this goal."

"Clients might bring us a diskette with a text file that has been word processed in a major word processor, such as WordPerfect or Microsoft Word, or they can bring us an ASCII file (a file that has been saved in a standardized coding scheme that lets computers and computer programs exchange information). We take their work and convert it into PageMaker or Ventura and help redesign the layout. We might change the fonts and the type size; we can add bullets or bold a subheading for emphasis. We might underline and italicize some parts, or clean up some areas, formatting in hanging indentations and borders. We do a spell check, too, because sometimes the clients' word processors don't have this feature."

A good service bureau will look for errors and even give advice on how to beef up your document. Usually there is a minimum cost for this professional assistance, varying from $15 to $25. Then you will pay an hourly rate, often about $30 per hour. Total cost of using such a service for "fixing up" a typical resume could range from $25 to $45. The cost of converting lengthy resumes, or vitae, can go even higher, as much as $100, or even more.

Whether you create the resume yourself, or turn this task over to a professional service, here are some examples:

- **Chronological** (see Figure 7.3)
- **Functional** (see Figure 7.4)

- **Linear** (see Figure 7.5)
- **Military** (see Figure 7.6)

These four resume formats contain much of the same information—they just provide a different focus. For example:

The *chronological* resume focuses on your job history.

The *functional* resume focuses on your abilities and accomplishments.

The *linear* resume is often a more detailed—customized for a specific company and industry—version of the functional format.

And finally, the *military* resume focuses on service history and accomplishments.

For more information on format descriptions and their uses, see Appendix B. There are other resume formats in use today, but these are, by far, the most popular and the most effective.

To use the resume styles listed above, you'll be taking advantage of many of your software's formatting features, such as bold, underline, italics, centering, borders, and so on. Don't be afraid to try these features—you can easily change them if you decide that you prefer another format.

When using the services of a desktop publishing professional or copy shop, be sure to indicate where you would like special underlining and borders to be placed. The more details that you give about what you want, the more comfortable you will feel with it. Ask for their professional suggestions, too.

Special resume programs include templates—generic worksheets—for special resume styles. Usually, you can tailor these templates to fit your needs. Tailoring a resume template, rather than building a resume from the ground up, is usually easier and quicker—you'll spend less time on headings and font styles.

Using Font Styles

Chances are, your word processor, desktop publishing package, or special resume software has a few font styles built in. If it doesn't, and you wish to add more creative type styles, you may want to invest in one of the many font packages available at most software stores.

Jeffery A. McAlley
5722 East Davis
St. Paul, MN 32115
(187)222-XXXX

OBJECTIVE: A position in Operations Management to include full responsibility for Procurement and Distribution in a medium-size manufacturing organization.

EXPERIENCE:

1987   **International Purchasing Inc., Dallas, TX** - *Operations Manager*
to   Administer daily operations including hiring and termination of
Present   personnel. Manage all buyers, assistant buyers, expediters, and trafficking
              personnel. Developed purchasing policies, procedures, and systems for
              profitable purchase of over 100,000 items. Company involved in
              purchasing, marketing, and distributing electronic components and parts
              for light and heavy equipment.

1985   **Lift Truck Services, Inc., Dallas, TX** - *Parts and Purchasing Manager*
to   Responsible for department operations. Established purchasing department,
1987   formulated policies, trained personnel, developed systems, and maintained
              quality control. Negotiated terms and conditions of contracts totaling $5.8
              million for factory dealerships.

1981   **ABC Rental, Dallas, TX** - *Assistant Store Manager*
to   Assisted in store operations including hiring, training, and
1985   supervising staff. Responsible for payroll, budget, and purchasing. Directly
              involved with purchase of $2 million equipment rental fleet.

EDUCATION: B.S., University of Texas, El Paso, 1981
                  Major: Business Administration
                  G.P.A. 3.6/4.0

REFERENCES: Available upon request.

Figure 7.3

A chronological resume developed with Works for Windows 2.0 word processing software on a PC, using Times New Roman 12 and 14 pt. type.

Figure 7.4

A linear resume developed with Word for Windows 2.0 word processing software on a PC using Caslon bold 12 and 14 pt. type, and Caslon normal.

Gary D. Patriot
6792 Your Street
El Paso, TX 79906
(915) 111-1111

Four years of responsible supply, operations, and human resources management experience. Energetic team player with documented success. Accomplished supervisor with outstanding skills in training, motivating, and team building.

Education

BBS University of Oregon, Eugene, Oregon
Major: Marketing, 1987
Activities: President, Marketing Club, 1984-1987
                   Varsity Basketball, 1984-1987

Advanced Officer Course, Ft. Bliss, Texas, 1992
Air Defense Officer Course, Ft. Bliss, Texas, 1988

Work History

9/90-Present   U.S. Army, Anybase, State - *Training Manager*
                         Responsible for planning and conducting training. Coordinates
                         extensively with Air Force and other Army units. Conducts
                         analysis and evaluation of training exercises for 500 soldiers.

2/90-6/90   U.S. Army, Someplace, Germany - *Supply Manager*
                         Directed Supply Management. Managed $500,000 budget.
                         Administered supply, storage, issue, and purchasing. Directed
                         staff of 12.

6/88-2/90   U.S. Army, Anybase, State - *Supply Supervisor*
                         Supervised 50 people. Responsible for $6 million worth of
                         equipment. Planned all training, maintenance, and supply.

Military Service

U.S. Army, Captain
Honorable Discharge, 1992

ARNOLD FASTBUCK
2311 FOXTROT LANE
SALT LAKE CITY, UTAH 84100
(804) 565-9709

SUMMARY

Seven years experience in performing a variety of accounting and financial functions for large corporations in Utah. Have served as Controller, problem solver, and consultant. Thoroughly knowledgeable in accounting computer applications.

MAJOR ACCOMPLISHMENTS

♦ As controller of ABC Enterprises, managed all accounting, company financing, and all employees in these fields.

♦ Developed system changes resulting in improved and quicker access to information and reports, resulting in reduced salaries by $100,000 per year.

♦ Established cash flow projection that assisted small company in avoiding insolvency.

♦ Set up automated accounting system at EFG Company that effectively tracked job costs.

EDUCATION

♦ B.A. Accounting, University of Utah, 1980

CERTIFICATION

♦ Certified Public Accountant, Utah, 1992

WORK HISTORY

ABC Enterprises, Salt Lake City, Utah - Controller (1988-1991)

EFG Company, Ogden Utah - Staff Accountant (1981-1984)

Bloomington International, Salt Lake City, Utah - Accounting Assistant (1980-1981)

Figure 7.5

A functional resume using Aldus PageMaker 4.0 desktop publishing on a PC, with Gothic bold 10 and 12 pt., Helvetica Narrow, 12 pt., and Wingdings, 10 pt.

Figure 7.6

A military resume using Resume & Job Search Pro, by PFS, with Cobb and Marin fonts, 12 and 14 pt.

SUSAN B. SHORT

**4391 Leigh Fisher Drive
Cleveland, OH 34098**

WORK HISTORY

1991 to Present
U.S. Army, Fort Anywhere, Texas
Senior Legal Non-Commissioned Officer

- Responsible for reviewing all investigative reports.

- Determines and drafts charges.

- Supervises and trains 12 employees.

- Senior point of contact--advises commanders.

- Exercises knowledge of civil and military law.

1985 to 1991
Non-Commissioned Officer in Charge

- Legal non-commissioned officer for large defense field office.

- Developed automated tracking system.

- Maintained law library, office and files.

EDUCATION

Troy State University
B.A. in Liberal Arts, 1982

MILITARY

U.S. Army, 1984 to Present
First Sergeant

TIP

A font package works along with your word processor to produce rich-looking text on your printer. Best of all, it works in the background, with nearly all dot-matrix, inkjet, and laser printers, and you usually don't even notice that it's there—until you print your masterpiece.

Although there are many font packages on the market today, a few may not work with your software. Be careful to choose the one that will support your word processor AND your printer. Two excellent programs that support most of the word processors, dot-matrix printers, inkjet printers, and laser printers on the market today are MoreFonts by Micrologic Software and LaserTwin by Metro Software.

- **MoreFonts by Micrologic Software**   MoreFonts creates fonts and type faces that are stored on your computer's hard drive. As you create your resume, you can see these type faces on your screen, and you can also reproduce them on any popular dot-matrix, inkjet or laser printer. MoreFonts also provides some creative special effects such as shadowing and texturing of your type faces. While this may not necessarily be useful in your resume, it might serve to get attention that you will create at some later time, and it will certainly be handy to have in your new position. Price Range: Low.

- **LaserTwin by Metro Software**   LaserTwin Software takes a rather unique approach when creating additional fonts. Like MoreFonts, LaserTwin is loaded from your computer's hard drive and operates in the background—you will never know it's there until you begin to print. LaserTwin makes your software thinks it's printing to a laser jet printer. LaserTwin certainly is an inexpensive alternative to costly laser printers. Price Range: Low.

Remember OnTime Software listed in Chapter 5? In order to produce all its reporting capabilities, you must have a laser printer. With the aid of LaserTwin, you can print all the great reports that are included in the OnTime program. There are several programs that benefit from LaserTwin's unique features. As with any computer product, check the package to see that the one you choose will work with your computer, printer, and other software.

When you *do* find the right font package for your word processor, be careful to use the various fonts sparingly. Unless you're applying for a position in graphic arts or advertising, stay away from the fancy fonts.

You should also be careful when mixing font sizes. You should stay with sizes that are easily readable by varying audiences—those who wear reading glasses—so that you can make your best possible impression. The most readable font sizes are 10 and 12 points. You can safely vary these sizes from 8 points for text to 14 points for major headings.

Some good font styles to use include: Times Roman, Courier, Prestige, and so on. These fonts will give your resume a crisp, professional look.

Publishing on the Desktop

Desktop publishing can be a very complex subject—many good books have been dedicated to the task of explaining this process. Though it's beyond the scope of this book to discuss much on desktop publishing, there are a few programs that you might want to experiment with if you are new to desktop publishing.

Here are a few programs you might want to try:

- **First Publisher by Spinnaker Software**   First Publisher is an excellent place for you to begin your first desktop publishing experience. It is powerful and easy to use, and its well-written manual can be used, in addition to the many good books available at your local bookstore. First Publisher does require a hard drive and can take advantage of the MoreFonts program. First Publisher is a low-priced product (less than $150).

- **Express Publisher by PowerUp Software**   Express Publisher, like First Publisher, is a powerful, yet easy-to-use program. This program requires a hard drive and can take advantage of several font programs like MoreFonts. Express Publisher is a low-priced product.

- **PageMaker by Aldus** (see Figure 7.5)   PageMaker, a program that is available for the PC, as well as the Macintosh, is an extremely powerful desktop publishing program. Though not always a good choice for the first-time user, the easier features of PageMaker can be learned in a very short amount of time. There are many fine manuals written about PageMaker at your local bookstore. It is a high-priced product (more than $350).

To keep your resume consistent, use the same font style throughout the entire document. If you use multiple font styles, it tires the reader before they get to the good stuff. The best advice from the publishing world is to keep it simple and consistent. Figure 7.5 is an example of a resume with all of the bells and whistles—using desktop publishing software. Notice the effective use of square bullets, lines, and special fonts.

TIP

To draw attention to a line or heading, try using a larger type size of the same font style, or use the italic feature. This is very effective, and keeps your resume focused.

Using A Resume For Maximum Results

Not every resume style is right for you or the position for which you're applying. And your job search certainly doesn't start and stop with resume preparation! In Appendices A and B, you'll find more help in conducting a successful job hunt written by Human Resource Specialist Elizabeth Smith. Included are sample resume formats and guidelines, cover letters, interviewing tips, as well as valuable networking advice.

After reviewing your document (don't forget to use your spell check feature), you're now ready to print.

Printing Your Resume

Now that you're ready to print that interview-winning resume, there are a few ground rules to be covered.

1. Avoid sending a resume printed on a dot-matrix printer without the aid of a program like LaserTwin. Remember the age-old adage: you never get a second chance to make a first impression. Never is that more important than in sending your resume.

2. If possible with your printer, use a top-quality bond paper, preferably one with a watermark. It should consist of 20% cotton, or more. If you do choose a watermarked bond, hold the watermark up to a light—the watermark should be right side up when your document is printed. This may seem like a very small detail, but prospective employers do notice them.

3. When using inkjet printers, be sure to allow time to let your document dry before folding it into an envelope.

4. You can always take your laser-printed original to a copy shop and have copies printed. They will have top-quality paper stock to choose from—order matching paper and envelopes!

Quick and Easy! Let's say you want a quick printer to typeset your two-page resume, provide laser output, print 100 copies on high-quality stock with a water-mark, provide 100 matching envelopes, and sell you 50 extra pages of matching stock and envelopes. One Midwest regional instant printing establishment gives this quote: $72 for typesetting ($36 per page), $17 for printing (17 cents per copy), $10.50 for the envelopes (7 cents per envelope), and $3.50 for the extra stock (7 cents per sheet). The total savings? $103!

Making Your Printer Look Better

If you're using a laser quality printer, your resume will look as if it were professionally typeset. If you're using a 9-pin dot-matrix printer, don't worry. There are several printer-enhancement programs available that make your printed copy look like laser quality.

Some good printer enhancement programs include:

- GoScript by Laser Go
- LaserTwin by Metro Software
- Image Printing Utilities by Image Computer Systems

GoScript makes your inkjet or dot-matrix printer think it's an Apple Laserwriter NT, with full postscript font capabilities.

LaserTwin makes your inkjet or dot-matrix printer think it's a HP Laserjet Series II, with full 300 DPI (that's dots per inch) resolution.

Image Printing Utilities (the pioneer of printer enhancement programs) makes your 9-pin dot-matrix printer think it's either a 24-pin or a laser printer, depending on the software settings.

If you don't see these program titles at your local software store, don't worry. They're worth requesting. Have the salesperson order a copy for you. Check the program before you make your purchase however, to be sure that your printer and word processor will work with that printer-enhancement program.

Using Commercial Printers

If you're not satisfied with the quality of your printer's output, as you've been shown in this chapter, you can plan a trip to your local "fast copier" shop or a printing service bureau. Many of these businesses now accept your documents on disk (provided you're using a software program from which they can import) and give you typeset-quality documents in a matter of minutes, while you wait.

If you feel you need the best possible quality in your resume appearance, this option might be for you. One word of caution, though: call ahead to see if they can import the document files you're creating.

Your Edge: Getting On-Line

In the past seven chapters, you learned how to use word processing, a data-base package, and other special software to enhance your job search. What you might not know is that your PC may have even more oomph—an ability to speed up your search close to the speed of light! In this chapter, you'll discover how your PC, a modem, and some special communications software can make a world of difference to your search.

Here's where you'll really get an edge on your job search. Using your PC and modem (a modem allows your PC to talk to other computers through the phone line), you can connect to on-line information services and receive valuable inside information about industries and companies—and their financial standings.

The services are already there, ready and waiting. Having this insight will allow you to make intelligent decisions about your career and will certainly impress the interviewer.

Getting Started

If you're new to the idea of getting on-line with your PC and modem, don't worry. Once you know what an on-line information service is, what it can do, and how to connect to it with your modem-equipped PC, you can navigate through it like a pro.

First, think of an on-line information service as a large computer database. In fact, it's an entire library (and more) that you can access with your PC. An on-line service can be a source for all sorts of information—from financial, statistical, and educational data to consumer reports and sports scores.

TIP

Some on-line services even let you shop at home, using your PC. Instead of driving all over town and walking from store to store, you can walk through the on-line services at the other end of your PC's keyboard.

On-Line Services Vary

Using an on-line information service isn't difficult to learn, at all. With most of the commercial services available today, you can be up and running in a matter of minutes. Once you get the hang of it, you'll want to spend hours at a time just looking at all the features. If you do, though, be careful to monitor how much you're spending in dollars, on-line.

There are many on-line information services available, each with a unique collection of databases (see Chapters 4 and 5 for more details). Some of the more popular services are:

- Prodigy (see Figure 8.1)
- CompuServe (see Figure 8.2)
- Dialog

Later in this chapter, you'll see what information is most important to your job hunt, so you can choose the best service (or services) to provide the needed information for your job search. With some careful comparisons, you can save both time and money.

Getting Access

How do you access an on-line information service? You may already have the answer filed away with your PC's user manuals.

If you've recently purchased your PC and modem, you may have received an introductory offer (and perhaps even the entire software package) included with the system. An introductory offer will usually include:

- A telephone access number.

- A user account number.

- A temporary password.

. . . or everything you need to get on-line immediately.

The Prodigy on-line service.

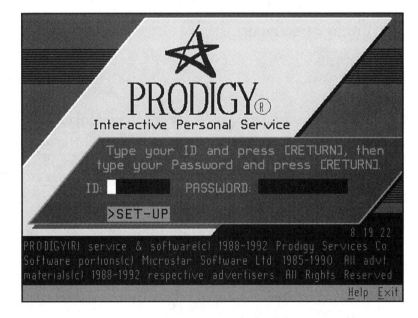

Other services may give you a customer service number to call (usually an 800 number). When you call this number, the service gives you all of the necessary access information, over the phone.

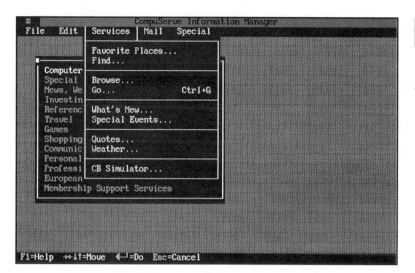

Figure 8.2

The CompuServe on-line service.

Once you have this information, you're ready to install or connect your modem and set up your telecommunications software.

- A modem is a piece of equipment that lets your PC talk to other computers.

- Telecommunications software controls the entire on-line process—from dialing-up to sending and receiving messages (also called data transfer).

Installing Your Modem

You'll need to install your PC's modem (if it didn't come already installed from the dealer). An internal modem is installed inside your PC, as explained in the product's installation instructions.

If you're going to use an external modem, you simply connect it to the serial port on the back of your PC using a serial cable (usually supplied with the modem).

Connecting To A Phone Line

Connect your PC to the telephone line by plugging one end of the line cord (the flat gray cable usually included with the modem) into the *telephone line* jack of the modem, and the other end of the line cord into the phone outlet. Now you're all set to install your telecommunications software. A dedicated modem line is helpful if you're doing a lot of on-line work.

Installing The Software

Because nearly every software program installs differently, consult the program manual for the proper installation procedure and the minimum system requirements. Many communications programs such as ProComm Plus, Microsoft Works, Eight-In-One, and so on, can be installed to run on a single 3 1/2-inch floppy disk, as well as on a hard disk. This makes them the ideal choice for use on laptops and portables, as well as smaller home computer systems.

Once you've installed your telecommunications software and loaded the program from your PC's keyboard, your screen may look similar to the one shown in Figure 8.3. This is the opening screen of ProComm Plus, the most widely used software of its kind in the industry.

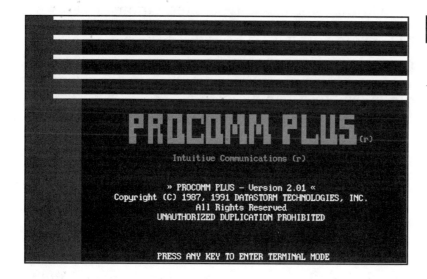

Figure 8.3

The opening screen of ProComm Plus.

TIP

If you haven't chosen a telecommunications program, take a look at ProComm Plus. It's easy to use and powerful.

Configuring (Setting Up Guidelines For) Your Software

Before you can use your telecommunications program to take your job hunt on-line, you need to configure (set some rules and guidelines) the software for your PC.

First, you'll need to know some techie-type information:

1. What is your PC's com port (COM1 or COM2)?

2. What is the baud, bits per second rate, for your modem?

3. What is your terminal type (if applicable)?

4. What are the required bit and parity bit values (if applicable)?

5. What is the required stop bit value (if applicable)?

- The *com port*, or communications port, is the address where the PC can locate and talk to the modem.

  If you're using a mouse, that device is usually connected to COM1, or communications port 1. *If you have an internal modem*, it usually has an internal COM2 address. If you're using a mouse, and you want to connect an external modem, you need TWO com ports on the rear of your PC. If you only have one serial port, it's best to buy an internal modem for your PC.

- The *baud rate* or *bps* (that's bits per second) *rate* of your modem determines how fast information travels in and out of your PC through the modem and phone line.

Just a few years ago, 300 baud used to be the standard. Now, most modems operate at 300, 1,200, and 2,400 baud. Some even move information at an incredible rate of 9,600 baud, and beyond!

TIP

Generally, when you consider the modem purchase price and the connect rates of many of the on-line information services, the 2,400 baud modem is the best value.

- The *terminal type* refers to how your PC looks at the information coming through the modem.

  This setting determines how your PC displays that information on the screen. There are many types of *emulations* (screen types) in use, but the most popular are the VT100 and the ANSI. Don't worry if you don't understand what these terms mean right now. You'll understand them better as you begin to use your modem with various services.

- *Data bit, parity,* and *stop bit* values are a little more complicated; they determine how the individual characters that you see on your screen are processed in your PC and modem.

The only thing you really have to understand about these values is that you must tell your modem (through your telecommunications software) what these values should be for each on-line service. In Figure 8.4, you can see how these settings are displayed in ProComm Plus. Most telecommunications programs handle these data bit, parity, and stop bit values in a similar manner.

Figure 8.4

Data bit, parity, and stop bit values displayed in ProComm Plus.

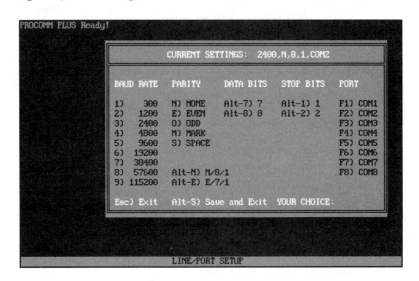

```
PROCOMM PLUS Ready!


            CURRENT SETTINGS:  2400,N,8,1,COM2


   BAUD RATE   PARITY      DATA BITS     STOP BITS    PORT

   1)    300   N) NONE    Alt-7) 7     Alt-1) 1     F1) COM1
   2)   1200   E) EVEN    Alt-8) 8     Alt-2) 2     F2) COM2
   3)   2400   O) ODD                               F3) COM3
   4)   4800   M) MARK                              F4) COM4
   5)   9600   S) SPACE                             F5) COM5
   6)  19200                                        F6) COM6
   7)  38400                                        F7) COM7
   8)  57600   Alt-N) N/8/1                         F8) COM8
   9) 115200   Alt-E) E/7/1

   Esc) Exit   Alt-S) Save and Exit  YOUR CHOICE:


                       LINE/PORT SETUP
```

Using Integrated Software

If you're using an integrated program like Microsoft Works or Eight-In-One, you have a telecommunications program built in. You'll find that it provides nearly all of the functions you need to get on-line and to send or receive information.

In Table 8.1, you can see how Microsoft Works is set up to operate like the ProComm Plus example in Figure 8.4. Now take a look at Table 8.2. You can see how these same settings look in Eight-In-One, which also contains telecommunications features similar to the ones in Microsoft Works. The actual words may vary, in some cases, but the concepts remain the same.

Table 8.1   Microsoft Works communications settings.

Baud rate	[2400]	Parity: (.) None	
Data bits:	(.)8	Port: (.)Com1	
Stop bits:	(.)1		
Handshake:	(.)Xon		

Table 8.2   Eight-In-One communications settings for data bit, parity, and stop bit values.

Port	Baud rate	Duplex
COM2	2400	FULL
Parity	*Data bits*	*Stop bits*
NONE	8	1

Using Commercial Services

Commercial information services, sometimes referred to as knowledge brokers, exist for the sole purpose of providing information to the customer. If you ever had any doubts as to whether we are in the information age, just browse through the ads—these ads tell you about their rates and how to join, their features, and their functions.

A few of the commercial information services require that you use their software to get on-line. Prodigy and America OnLine are good examples of this kind of software-specific information service. Other services that only recommend the use of their software, but don't actually require its use, include CompuServe and Dialog.

When shopping for an on-line service, you should weigh the cost and the depth of information you'll be able to access. The on-line charges can range anywhere from $7.95 per month for CompuServe's basic services, to nearly $300 per hour for some of Dialog's professional databases.

See Table 8.3 for current, basic on-line access rates for Prodigy, CompuServe, and Dialog. Whatever the cost, though, you can bet it'll be worth the time and effort once you get that new job!

Table 8.3   On-line information services, basic access rates.

Prodigy	$14.95 / Month
CompuServe	$ 7.95 / Month
	$12.00 / Hour
Dialog	$12.00 / Hour

PRODIGY Prodigious! You can use PRODIGY services for faxing, electronic mail, and U.S. Postal Services. PRODIGY has recently expanded services including strengthened investor features, support of 9,600-bps access, links to worldwide Internet, an international network for education and research, and enhanced E-mail options. Members can send messages they compose off-line as faxes or first-class letters for an additional charge based on the length of the correspondence. Financial features range from Dow Jones News/Retrieval to the ability to pull quotes on more than 50 market indices, statistics, and key indicators.

Researching Industries And Companies

Now that you know how to set up your modem to tap into on-line information services, you should consider which information services contain the databases you need for your job hunt. Here's an overview of some of the more valuable databases you can use to conduct your on-line job hunting research:

- **Standard & Poors**   S&P gives you a good overview of a company by telling you its financial ranking, sales volume, company summary, and so on.

Use S&P regularly to see how specific companies within an industry are doing.

- **Dun & Bradstreet**   D&B reports tell you about financial standings and whether a company is stable. D&B also lists officers of the company, complete addresses and phone numbers, and any activity such as plant expansions (very useful for filling in your "comments" field).

- **Dow Jones**   Dow Jones will not give you an overview, but it is helpful in determining if a company's stock profile is going up or down. This will be handy in determining what companies to target in your search.

Because Standard & Poors, Dun & Bradstreet, Dow Jones, and dozens of other informative databases are available on several commercial information services such as CompuServe and Dialog, you should spend some time comparing these information services to find the best collections for you. It will probably mean that you'll have to subscribe to several services to get the kind of information you'll need to get the better job offer.

If you choose CompuServe, a typical path to find a company's earnings projections, S&P, overview and economic outlook would begin at the General Services menu, where you would select the Money Matters option. The Money Matters option then leads to another set of menus, and helps you narrow your search down to the specific overview and economic outlook information you need on that particular company.

Bulletin Boards: Today's Electronic Corkboards

Bulletin Board Systems (BBSs) are great tools for your job search. They're a place where professionals congregate to send notes to one another.

How do you tap into a BBS? Several publications print BBS telephone numbers. The best single-source directory for BBS numbers from around the country is *Online Access.* Online Access lists many of the BBS services provided nationwide in the area of employment such as:

- OPM, Newark, NJ

    Specializes in federal positions. Their phone number is 201/645-3887.

- JobTrac Jobs Network, Dallas, TX

    This is an employment service that exchanges resumes. Their phone number is 214/349-0527.

- Career Connection, Aurora, CO

    This is an employment database service. Their phone number is 303/671-0801.

For more employment listings like the ones listed above, you can get a copy at your local bookstore or software dealer. *Online Access* also lists the available databases offered by many of the commercial information services. Also see Appendix D for additional listings of commercial and bulletin board on-line services.

When connecting to a BBS for the first time, here are the settings you should use:

- 2,400 Baud
- Even Parity
- 7 Bits
- One Stop Bit

If all this technical jargon is confusing to you, ask a friend who is familiar with modems and their set-up to help you, or call your local computer store.

If you connect to the nationwide BBS JobTrac, for example, you can pull up information on select cities, such as Dallas, TX. You'll then have options to select educational bulletins, register with employers, enter a "quick" resume, enter or read messages, and more. Employers are given an opportunity to locate resumes in a special directory and download any resumes of their choice.

Forums and Special Interest Groups

Forums and Special Interest Groups (SIGs) allow you to get fresh, inside information about all sorts of companies and industries. They work much like a BBS, but you'll be communicating "live" from your keyboard to others from around the country—or around the world. This is where you can network with others in your field and get those valuable job leads.

Getting on-line with your PC is perhaps the most valuable source of information you'll ever gain. No other resource provides you with as much timely information valuable to your job hunting efforts as your on-line service.

In Chapter 9, you'll discover another aspect of getting on-line—how to send your qualifications using your modem and PC.

Presenting Your Qualifications: On-Line

How do you suppose your data-communicated self will be seen by other people—the folks at the end of the telephone line? In face-to-face communication, people generally judge other people very quickly—and not always reasonably or fairly. Eye contact, the strength of a handshake, even personal distance all decide how we perceive others. Do on-line resumes have any advantage? Your words and content will hit first—before you ever have to shake a hand!

Presenting The Paperless Resume!

The popularity of PCs brings a new way to present your qualifications to a possible employer—the electronic resume.

This resume doesn't look like the resume that you would print on paper. Instead, it's a listing of your qualifications, experiences, and education, uniquely formatted to be sent via modem to a company's database or an on-line information service.

TIP

Keep your hard copy format intact for faxing and mailing application letters and resumes.

Sending (or transmitting) your resume electronically gives prospective employers instant access to your background and work history and lets them collect and sort candidates with the speed and accuracy that can only come from using a PC. Your advantage is one of speed—you can reach more people in less time using this electronic means of sending your resume.

Some Techie Rules For Transmission's Sake

Rules? Rules! How can we do techie stuff without techie rules? So here are a couple of simple guidelines to follow when sending your electronic resume:

1. Prepare your resume for transmission using ASCII files (standardized file text format that can be exchanged between most computers).

2. Check with the prospective employer, or on-line information service, where you're going to be transmitting your document. Ask what format to use, and how long the document should be.

Reasons For The Techie Rules

You don't have to rewrite the whole document, you just can't send it in its present form. To understand why, take a look at the resume file shown in Figure 9.1. All the strange looking characters on the screen are the formatting codes your word processor uses to enhance your resume—the bold, italic, and underlining features used to make your resume stand out from the crowd.

While these features served you well in producing an impressive printed resume, formatting codes can cause problems when you transmit your resume to a prospective employer's database, or to an on-line information service.

Most databases and information services can only handle document files that are sent in a *standardized file text format.* In other words, you can only use the alphanumeric characters on your keyboard (A,a,B,b,1,2, and so on) without the graphic characters (borders and so on) and the formatting characters used by your word processor. You're also limited to only one font—Courier 10. For a glimpse at what your electronic resume should look like, see Figure 9.2.

Because your electronic resume will appear in the same general format as everyone else's, aren't you glad you took the extra effort in Chapter 7 to build a personal worksheet—making sure you stand out in content, even when you're forced to look like everybody else?

Figure 9.1

A resume complete with formatting codes.

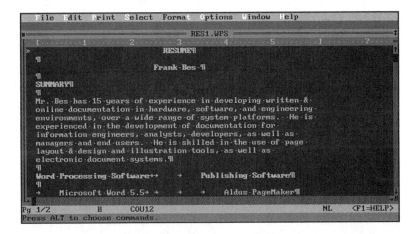

Figure 9.2

A resume in ASCII format.

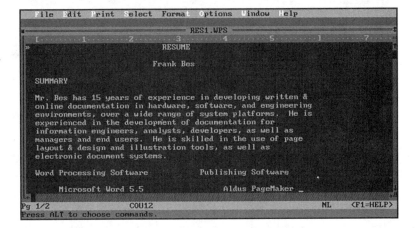

Most databases and on-line information services must receive and display your resume in ASCII. Carefully create and save the file in a form that's free of any special features—or formatting codes.

If you're not sure your text is being edited and saved in an ASCII format, try using the "print to disk file" feature (if your word processor has one) to create your electronic resume. This will nearly always produce a pure ASCII text file.

You can "export" the resume file in a "text only" format. This will give you the same results as "printing to disk," even though it might require an extra step or two on your part. Consult your word processor manual's index under ASCII Text, or Export, to find the right procedure for your software.

When you develop your electronic resume, check with the prospective employer, or on-line information service to which you're going to be transmitting your document. They'll tell you what format to use, and how long the document should be.

Electronic Resume Services

Currently, there are several places (a few, but powerful!) where you can send your resume electronically—and the list is growing monthly. For a more complete list of available services including their telephone number, see Appendix D in the back of this book. Here are a few of the services you may want to check out initially:

- **Adnet Online**   vendors: CompuServe, PRODIGY, America Online, PC-LINK, Promenade, BIX (Byte Information Exchange) and GEnie (General Electric Corp.).

- **Career Placement Registry**   vendor: Dialog.

- **OPM**   a BBS listing federal employment positions.

- **JobTrac Jobs Network**   Texas, employment service BBS.

- **Career Connection**   Colorado, employment service BBS.

- **Various Professional Organizations**   some have a BBS job bank section, especially for displaying resumes.

Adnet Online can give your search a high-tech boost (GO ADNET on CompuServe and Jump ADNET on PRODIGY). On Compu-Serve, you'll find Adnet on the employment advertising network available on the Classifieds menu (Select Option 1, "Browse/Read Ads").

With hundreds of prestigious employers such as Motorola Corp., Digital Equipment Corp., MasterCard International, H&R Block, Shearson Lehman and a number of federal government agencies offering professional, managerial and technical job listings online, Adnet can be an efficient way to locate a job. You might find jobs listed with the Internal Revenue Service, the U.S. Department of Commerce, the U.S. Post Office, or even the Central Intelligence Agency, as well!

According to Adnet's president, Al Wigginton, scanning these well-categorized ads can save you money at a time when money counts. "You can spend $14 in a heartbeat buying Sunday newspapers and trade magazines, and you can spend a lot of hidden dollars in a search that lasts weeks or months because you forget about that trip to the bookstore or the drive to the library downtown. With Adnet, we're creating a central repository for important positions, which users can read at their leisure."

Designed for those actively looking for employment, as well as those who want to track hiring trends in specific industries, Adnet Online allows you to search by type of position and geographical location. Listings, which are lengthy and detailed since there are no space limitations, are displayed as soon as a position becomes available and removed once they are filled. In addition, the majority of the jobs listed in Adnet Online do not appear in newspaper classifieds, offering you a leg up on the competition. According to an Adnet spokesman,

Adnet posts as many as 1,500 positions at a given time, representing up to 1,000 corporate clients. Jobs are updated twice weekly. Many positions, he added, are specific to newly retired military personnel.

Adnet also offers an electronic resume service. Recruiters can dial in and complete a key word search on Adnet, at no charge. Cost of placing a resume on the service is $24.50 and the resume stays on the system for six months. Adnet accepts any resume format, because they will put the resume into their own format, once it is received. Use of key words in the resume is critical. The Adnet spokesman suggests using specific language in areas of education and expertise. "Use 'COBOL,' or 'C+,' not 'programming languages' and give specific titles, such as systems analyst."

Career Placement Registry contains over 25,000 resumes of both recent college graduates and experienced professionals. Your resume is kept on file for six months, ready for viewing by any of Dialog's thousands of subscribers. This database is also used extensively by personnel managers and headhunters.

Other on-line services, such as OPM, JobTrac Jobs Network, and Career Connection, are great places to let your resume do your talking for you. Their access numbers are listed in Appendix D.

There are thousands of BBSs in operation nationwide. For the best listing, and a thorough explanation of the services they provide, buy a copy of *Online Access* at your local computer bookstore. This magazine is updated quarterly with the latest revised listings.

Professional Groups BBS

Other good, but often overlooked, sources of quality BBS services are professional associations and societies. These organizations often maintain a BBS for members to post their talents.

For instance, the Society for Technical Communication has a bulletin board which posts jobs, as well as resumes, for technical writers and documentation specialists. If you belong to a professional organization—if you don't, you should—check to see if that organization offers a BBS.

Many local chapters, as well as national headquarters, provide a BBS and the necessary assistance you may need to use it effectively. When you're looking for a new job, this service alone can be worth the cost of annual dues.

Major Companies Accepting On-Line Resume

Some major companies are now starting to accept electronic resumes and have separate telephone lines installed to receive your document. Call them first, check their procedure, and stress personal confidentiality before sending your qualifications to a larger corporation.

This kind of telephone call frequently reveals the option to send the resume file electronically, if the employer uses the software with which you created the file. For example, if the employer can take resumes in WordPerfect format, you can then send, by modem, your WordPerfect file. The advantages are the same as from faxing.

> **TIP**
>
> *Sometimes good networking can come back to haunt you—especially if you don't want your boss to know you're looking for another job. Know where you're sending an electronic resume and how it will be used.*

How Will Someone See My Resume?

Here's how most human resource databases work. When prospective employers have a job opening, they can sort through the thousands of resumes in their databases to find the top three to six candidates to bring in for the interviews.

It almost makes you feel as if you've been reduced to a "byte" on some PC's hard drive, doesn't it? Well don't worry. Because you took the time to work on the content of your resume in Chapter 7, you'll still stand out from the rest.

Job hunting can be somewhat of a numbers game—the more exposure you have, the better your chances of finding the job that's right for you. Try to use as many of the resources listed in this chapter (and this book, for that matter) to improve your chances of finding the right opportunity.

Word Processing and Databases: Coming Together

In this book, you've learned a lot of techie stuff to help move you along the job hunting path. (This chapter's no exception—you'll see how to strengthen your database and to merge word processing and database files to create personalized letters.) Yet, here's some other important, nontechie counsel: every so often, sit back in your chair for a moment or two, take in a big breath, let it out slowly, relax, and think good thoughts about yourself. Enjoy the moment. . . . Then get back to work! There are good jobs out there—waiting just for you!

Buddy Up Your Software!

Now's the time to unleash the power of your PC! By expanding the structure of your database and adding some new facts and figures, you can merge all of this information with your word processor, creating attention-getting form letters and reminding yourself of follow-up details.

Plus, during an interview, it will be more than apparent you've done your research! Employment counselors say you have the edge in an interview when you can speak intelligently about the interviewing company.

Fattening Up Your Database with New Facts and Figures

In Chapter 6, you saw how to set up a basic, workable database. Then, in Chapter 8, you learned how to tap into valuable, but little known, resources. (Using your PC and modem, you learned how to connect to on-line information services and receive valuable inside information about industries and companies—and their financial standings.) Use these powerful tools together, and you can start filling your database with even more vital information for your job search.

Begin by entering all of the background information that you re-trieve from the Standard & Poors, Dun & Bradstreet, and Dow Jones reports, on a daily basis. Then, get any additional information on job leads from bulletin board systems and special interest groups. Remember, the more contacts you make by networking, the quicker and easier it will be to get the job.

TIP

Since you'll be filling your database at a rather rapid rate, don't forget to back up your files by following the procedures found in your software guide. There are several good back-up programs that make this task quick and easy, such as FASTBACK Plus by Fifth Generation Systems (moderately priced) and Central Point Backup by Central Point Software (low priced).

You'll probably need to modify your database structure (create some more fields) in your database. Data loss is always a concern when modifying the structure. (If, for instance, you are changing a date-type field to alphanumeric, you'll no longer be able to perform date arithmetic, which can be a significant loss. Yet, there may be times when you want dates in a format your database doesn't support.) Be sure you have good backups before starting such a project. Different software requires you to use export and import features in different ways to minimize the loss of data.

Making Changes   *Users of Paradox database software are instructed that they can change a field's data without losing information if they change from number to currency, currency to number, date to alphanumeric, alphanumeric to date (if the field contains only dates in one of Paradox's approved formats), or alphanumeric to numeric, and vice versa (if the field contains only numerals). Any other type changes will result in an error message.*

Here are some ways that you can track information more thoroughly, by filling your database with facts and figures you pick up from your on-line service searches:

- **Tracking facts and figures from Standard & Poors**

1. Create a new field in your database structure called "industry" and track *specific types* of industries.

By using this field, you can track companies within a group, like health care, avionics, architectural, banking, and so on. This way, when you compose form letters, you can "batch" your information and create a letter geared toward that industry.

As your database gets larger, create a new database file for each indus-try that you want to track. This can save you sorting time.

2. Build a "division" or "department" field in your database structure.

No doubt, you'll come across some rather large corporations with more than one division. For instance, a financial corporation will have trust, loan, and real estate divisions.

Create a separate field to track the officer in charge, so you can send your correspondence directly to that person. Although large companies may have one central human resources department, it's usually the manager or officer of each division that decides who gets hired. With that in mind, set up a "division, manager" field and use that field, in addition to your "division" or "department" field.

- **Tracking facts and figures from Dun & Bradstreet**

1. Add a "D & B ratings" field to your database structure.

This new field will help you keep information on the rankings that D & B assigns to a company. This is a great way to zero in on those companies you wish to target in your job search. By using this field and the sort function on your database, you can list only those compa-nies above a specific D & B rating.

2. Create a "prior activity" field.

D & B is a wonderful tool because it gives you an overview of what's happening inside that company. By creating a "prior activity" field, you'll not only have the company's ratings, but you'll also be able to tell something of their past history. Allow some space for this field, as it may become a little lengthy.

If your database will allow it, expand this field to about 30 to 40 spaces. Put in information such as "expanded plant to 40,000 sq. ft. in April, 1990." You may want to include this in correspondence later, so keep that in mind when filling in this field.

3. Add a "future plans" field.

A future plans field can be used as a measuring tool to see where the company is headed. Although this information may not always be available, it will certainly be valuable if you have captured it on your database. Include enough room so all the information is at your finger-tips.

The information you'll put in this field may contain "plans for new five story office development in 1993." Again, you may want to include this in your correspondence, so be sure to word this field carefully.

- **Tracking facts and figures from Dow Jones**

1. Set up "opening" and "closing" fields.

Although the Dow Jones will only give you opening and closing figures, this information, used over time, can prove to be very valuable. For instance, if you were able to trace a company's stock activity over a period of time, you would be able to determine if that company was on a growth track. However, you must set up several fields to track the trends that a company goes through in a period of time (maybe a month, or a quarter).

How long you want to track a company's stock activity is up to you. Set up enough fields to track accurate information. Your fields may be labeled: "open 1/3" (for opening figures of January 3) and "close 1/3" (for closing figures of January 3).

Then, in your form letter, or correspondence, you can mention the recent closing figure (if it is favorable). If so, simply merge that information directly into the body of the letter.

TIP

The use of figures and statistics in a letter or during an interview creates quite an impression on a prospective employer. Your on-line services can give you the facts you'll need.

> **TIP**
>
> *If you really want to follow the Dow Jones more in-depth, there are several programs available that will allow you to conduct a more sophisticated tracking system.*

Any additional information that you think might be useful should be added to your database. Remember, you can never have too much information. (Well, hardly ever!)

Tips from Ed McMahon's School of Form Letters

After you fill in your database with new facts and figures, create a form letter for use in producing your cover letters. Form letter, you say! That's the kind of stuff Ed McMahon sends out!

Actually, the answer is "no." It's obvious that Ed's letters are fresh off the computer. Sophisticated form letters are personalized—they look like regular letters—and they can save you tons of time. In fact, you can produce several personalized letters in a matter of minutes, simply by using your database and word processor together.

With an integrated program, merging your database and word processor is an easy task, because you never leave the one software program. Some resume programs offer the same easy merge capabilities of a fully integrated program.

Setting Up Your Form Letter

Read your software manual's section on form letters. Each program has its own set of instructions. Generally, to create a form letter, open a new document file on your word processor.

If you're not sure what kind of form letter would be appropriate, see Appendix A.

You may want to date your letter or simply use the first field on your job hunt database to fill in the first line. Next, merge the Mr/Mrs/Ms, First Name, Last Name, and Title fields on one line—remember to use the exact field names.

On the second line, merge Address 1. Merge Address 2 on the third line, and on the fourth line, merge the City, State, and Zip Code fields. Include a comma after the City field, and add the appropriate spaces between State and Zip Code fields.

On the salutation line, type **Dear**, and then directly behind that, merge the "Mr/Mrs/Ms" and "Last Name" fields, followed by a semicolon.

TIP

Because databases can't read your mind, you must put in the appropriate punctuation and spacing requirements.

In the body of the letter, refer to the job that you're interested in by merging the Position field. See the example in Figure 10.1 for a step-by-step merging process using Microsoft Works as an example.

To create form letters to target certain cities or zip codes, it's a good idea to sort your database first. Sorting your database will help ensure that you'll get only the information that you request, not all of the records in the entire database.

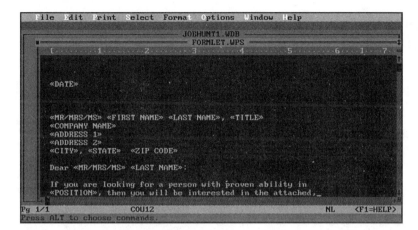

File Edit Print Select Format Options Window Help

JOBHUNT1.WDB
FORMLET.WPS

«DATE»

«MR/MRS/MS» «FIRST NAME» «LAST NAME», «TITLE»
«COMPANY NAME»
«ADDRESS 1»
«ADDRESS 2»
«CITY», «STATE» «ZIP CODE»

Dear «MR/MRS/MS» «LAST NAME»:

If you are looking for a person with proven ability in
«POSITION», then you will be interested in the attached._

Pg 1/1   COU12   NL   <F1=HELP>
Press ALT to choose commands.

Figure 10.1

A form letter template with the fields displayed.

With most database programs, you can sort your information in several ways, selecting the fields that you want to see. You may select a field you want sorted and, depending on what is contained in the field, sort it alphabetically from a to z (or z to a), or numerically (in ascending or descending order). This is an easy process, which only takes a few moments to complete.

When you've inserted the fields that you want to display in your form letter, the template will look a bit different than regular form letters that are type-written. The fields will be displayed in either brackets (<<first name>>) or asterisks (*first name*). Do not be alarmed—the field names will be replaced by real data that is merged from your database, and the finished product will look just like a regular form letter.

Print Those Letters!

After you've finished sorting your database, creating your form letter, and merging your fields, you're ready to print those all-important cover letters. Some programs, such as Microsoft Works have a special form letter printing feature that simplifies this process. Many resume programs let you print using a simple function key. Your finished product may look like the example in Figure 10.2.

Figure 10.2

A finished form letter.

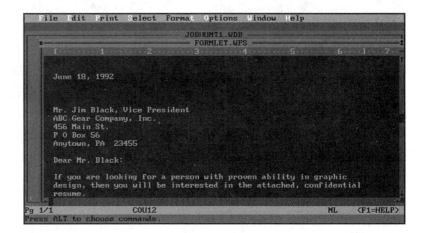

Getting a Tickle from Your Database

Your follow-up will be well organized when you use your PC for tickling. Come on, you shouldn't need a definition for tickler—it's a reminder that comes to you on a special date and time. You might need a tickle, for instance, to help you remember to send a thank-you note after an interview.

Now that you're familiar with database applications, personal organizers, and resume programs, you can follow up all of your job leads with ease.

Here's an example of how you can use your database on a typical follow-up application:

It's the weekend and you are going to relax and watch a game on TV. While you are watching the game, you can have your database sort by date order to get a listing of the interviews or contacts that you have had during the last week or two to generate correspondence for the week.

You can relax while your computer does the task of sorting through the many records you have in your database. Then, once the sorting is done, you can merge your current information with a form letter on your word processor, set up your printer, and generate your week's correspondence in no time.

Open your database and use your sort command to sort data in your follow-up date field.

Because your sort field is a numeric field (using all numbers instead of letters), tell your database to sort in ascending or descending order. Choose ascending to choose the earliest date.

If your database has the capability, you may want to sort between two specific days. This way the database will give you only a few days at a time in a list.

Now that you have retrieved a specific follow-up date or dates, use this information to make regular follow-up calls or letters.

You can get all the tickles you want from project management or time management software, besides from your database. These programs provide reminders and a calendar of events. Some resume programs have handy reminder tools for you to use.

With such a wealth of information as close as your keyboard, spend some time each day with on-line research, correspondence, follow-up, and planning.

With your PC, you'll be amazed at how little time and effort it takes to conduct a successful job search and to find a challenging job, offering a rewarding career.

Other Resources for Your Job Search

Throughout this book, you've learned how to use your PC to become more successful in a job search. This section of the book provides more details about the software you can use in a job search (Appendix A) and on-line services and bulletin board services (Appendix D) that list employment opportunities or enable you to network to generate job leads.

Appendixes B and C provide information from a human resource professional about how you can make yourself more competitive in the job market. Learn how to prepare for an interview, how to deal with interview questions (even difficult ones), and how to select the appropriate resume format.

Helpful Software and Books

In this index, you'll find the names of wonderful books and super software that will help move your job search into action!

Software that Makes it Happen

Following is information about some of the most popular application packages — all of which offer you features that can make your job search more productive and efficient. All software mentioned in this appendix is given even greater coverage in specific chapters of *Job Hunting With Your PC*.

Database Software (Chapter 1)

> *MyDatabase by MySoftware* can be run on a single floppy disk drive computer, and can easily be customized for your specific job search needs.

PRO: This package is one of the few currently available that can be run on older systems. It's a good choice if your computer doesn't have a hard drive or has limited memory.

Address Book Plus by PowerUp Software is available for both DOS-based personal computers and Macintosh computers. Address Book Plus will operate on a single floppy drive computer. It offers easy-to-learn sorting and import/export features. It enables you to perform mail merges with many popular word processing formats. Address Book Plus can print your information so you can put it in a Day Timer or Day Runner personal organizer. You also can print mailing labels on pre-perforated Avery label stock. CON: This program is primarily an address list, and is therefore limited in what it offers. It is not a good choice if you need to customize your database, or want to organize other kinds of information.

Rolodex Plus by Avery Software can be run off of a floppy or hard drive, and is capable of creating an address book that can be inserted into a Rolodex Datebook Organizer. CON: This package also is not a full-featured database. Choose it only if your computer has no hard drive or limited memory, or if you don't need to manage information besides names and addresses.

Microsoft Works by Microsoft Corporation See its listing under "Integrated Software Packages."

dBase IV 1.5 by Borland needs a hard drive and plenty of memory, and is designed for use by someone who has some computing experience. PRO: dBase has long been one of the database standards of the industry. This version is fully compatible with older versions. It offers a user-friendly Control Center and can handle a virtually unlimited number of entries. CON: Higher in price ($795) and complex, this program may be overkill and too difficult for a beginner to use effectively.

FoxPro is a relational database (which means it can work with data from two tables, or databases, at once). Like dBase, it requires a hard drive and plenty of memory. It's similar to dBase but runs substantially faster. CON: The price ($395 for the PC version and $495 for the Mac version) may be prohibitive if you want it for personal use only.

Paradox by Borland is a relational database for the PC. Made to be easy-to-use, Paradox offers more features than the average user will ever access, including queries-by-example which make it easier to find data, and customizeable reports. CON: Despite the fact that it's touted to be "easy," Paradox beginners face a relatively steep learning curve. The price ($795) makes it a better choice for corporate use. PRO: Paradox can manage virtually any kind of information. You can also create scripts (which are like macros) to automate repetitive tasks, increasing its ease-of-use.

Windows Cardfile Utility by Microsoft Corporation comes as an accessory with both Windows 3.0 and 3.1. Each record appears on-screen in a 3 x 5 card format. Cards are simple to add. CON: There's little opportunity to customize Cardfile for your needs, and you can't create custom reports, print labels, or merge data. PRO: If you're a Windows user, Cardfile is not a bad choice for managing a contact list. It's free (since you bought Windows anyway), and it lets you copy card contents into other Windows application documents.

Word Processing Software (Chapter 2)

Microsoft Word by Microsoft Corporation is available for DOS (Version 5.5), Windows (Version 2.0), and Mac (Version 5.0). This robust word processor has been one of the most popular over the past few years. It offers convenient features such as mail merge, outlining, spell checking, and thesaurus, as well as excellent text-formatting capabilities. The Windows version offers drawing, charting, and desktop publishing features, too. This is a good all-around choice for a word processing program. CON: At $395 to $495, Word may cost more than your budget allows. PRO: It's easy to share files between the Mac and PC versions of Word, as well as to import ASCII (plain text) files. The formatting features are also relatively easy to master. You can display your text formatting on-screen to see how the document will look when printed.

WordPerfect 5.1 by WordPerfect Corporation should be installed on a hard drive. Windows and Mac versions of this, the best-selling word processor, are also available. WordPerfect is robust, and offers most of the same features (and some others) as Word. It costs up to $495. CON: WordPerfect uses a fairly complicated menu system. Many users rely on a keyboard template to learn how to navigate through the program. PRO: There are few things that WordPerfect can't do. And, because many companies use WordPerfect, learning it can be an asset in a job search.

PFS: Write by Spinnaker Software operates on a hard drive system, and requires no additional memory. It is the only DOS-based word processor that offers true WYSIWYG (What-You-See-Is-What-You-Get) on-screen presentation of your document. It offers basic graphics and drawing tools, as well as a spell checker, grammar checker, thesaurus, outliner, and clip art to spice up your documents. PRO: The $129 price tag makes this package a good bargain for the features it offers.

WordStar by WordStar International is available for both DOS and Windows, and should be installed on a hard drive. This package is not as popular as it once was. It offers features similar to Word and WordPerfect.

Ami Pro 3.0 by Lotus Development Corporation runs under the Windows environment and is not available for the Macintosh. This word processor's rich graphics handling makes it more like a desktop publishing application than any other word processor described here. It not only handles multi-column documents with ease, but allows you to place text and graphics in special frames that let you customize their placement. In addition to its spell checking, grammar checking, and thesaurus, Ami Pro enables you to create indexes, outlines, and tables of contents. CON: Though paying up to $495 for this package is reasonable considering its capabilities, it may offer more than you need. PRO: Ami Pro's basic features are easy to use. And, the latest version offers a streamlined Merge! feature that not only lets you create a merge document, but also create and store a merge data file.

Windows Write by Microsoft Corporation is included in Windows 3.0 and 3.1 for IBM-compatible systems. It offers basic word processing features, including simple editing and formatting. CON: Write doesn't offer a merge feature, although you can easily paste in data from other Windows applications. PRO: If you have Windows, you have Write, and it may offer enough formatting features to meet your needs.

Integrated Software Packages (Chapter 3)

Microsoft Works by Microsoft Corporation is an integrated program that has a database module. Works is available in DOS, Windows, and Macintosh versions. It can create listings that can be merged with its own word processor, so it's a very convenient package to use. PRO: For the price ($149-$249, depending on which version you buy), Works offers a lot of power and is simple to use.

PFS: First Choice by Spinnaker Software has sold over half a million copies since it was introduced. Offered for IBM-compatible systems only, this $149 package offers basic capabilities in word processing, databases, spreadsheets, mail merges, and communications. It's a good all-around choice, particularly if your system has limited capabilities.

Microsoft Windows 3.1 by Microsoft Corporation will require a hard drive to operate, and quite a bit of memory. It's really an operating environment rather than an integrated package, but it does offer Cardfile (a simple database), Write (a basic word processor), and Terminal (a communications interface). CON: Don't buy Windows as an integrated package—the capabilities are too limited. Simply remember that it has features that can fill a need when you don't have other resources. PRO: Windows Accessories are easy to use, and its graphical user interface (GUI) makes creating documents more intuitive. It also facilitates linking information between applications, such as pasting spreadsheet data into a word processing document.

Resume Software (Chapter 4)

PFS:Resume & Job Search Pro by Spinnaker Software is a sophisticated, easy to use program that not only combines resume formats, but will help you track your contacts and keep organized. PFS:Resume Pro & Job Search works best with a hard drive.

Expert Resume by Expert Software is a very easy to use program and includes sample resume designs that can be customized. This program supports either a dual floppy PC or a hard drive PC.

Key Resume Writer by Softkey Software Products, Inc. requires the use of your word processor to operate, but works well with many word processors. You will need a PC with a hard drive.

Personal Productivity Software (Chapter 5)

OnTime by Campbell Services, Inc. can be run on a floppy or hard drive system, with both DOS ($69.95) and Windows ($129.95) versions available. While it does support a dot matrix printer, its unique three-fold printout is available only on a laser printer. This combination appointment book, to-do list, desktop planner, tickler file, and alarm clock can be valuable if you need help getting organized. Its attractive, graphical screens and calendar printouts make it easy to learn and depend on.

Calendar Creator Plus by PowerUp Software can be run on a floppy or hard drive IBM-compatible and supports laser, ink-jet, and dot-matrix printers. Track meetings, special events, birthdays, and other dates you need to remember. Create calendars in daily, monthly, or yearly formats. At $59.95, the price is reasonable but may be more than you want to spend to keep track of dates and times.

Microsoft Windows Calendar by Microsoft Corporation requires a hard drive and supports laser, ink-jet and dot-matrix printers. Calendar offers an alarm feature and can run in the background along with your other applications. CON: There's not much to customize here, and the printouts may not be in the format you prefer. PRO: It comes as part of Windows 3.0 or 3.1, and may be the cheapest alternative for you.

Some Good Books

There are many books, pamphlets and other publications out there—waiting to help you with your job search. Some of the books may be purchased inexpensively at a bookstore. Others will probably be available at your library. Most libraries, these days, have inter-library loan systems, so if you can't find a book, just ask a friendly librarian. Be sure and ask for the most recent editions!

Some Classic Resources

Billion Dollar Directory: America's Corporate Families. Dunn & Bradstreet: New York, NY. This book lets you see companies alphabetically, geographically, and by product. Various divisions and subdivisions of major corporations are listed.

Standard & Poor's Register of Corporations, Directors and Executives. Standard & Poor's, McGraw-Hill: New York, NY. This favorite comes in three volumes. You'll find information on major companies by industry and geography, as well as details and contact information on companies.

Thomas Register of American Manufacturers. Thomas Publishing Company: New York. This is an enormous set of big green books found in nearly any reference section of a library or in offices of any manufacturing businesses. There are literally thousands of large and small companies listed in these books.

Some Lesser Known Guides

Career Development Opportunities for Native Americans. Office of Indian Educational Programs, Bureau of Indian Affairs: Department of the Interior, Washington, D.C.

Career Guide to Professional Associations: A Directory of Organizations by Occupational Field. Carroll Press: Cranston, RI.

Women Helping Women: A State by State Directory of Services. Women's Action Alliance: New York, NY.

Other Helpful Books

- General

What Color is Your Parachute 1992? Richard B. Bolles wrote this classic. Ten Speed Press. ISBN 0-89815-440-5.

The Ex-Inmates' Complete Guide to Successful Employment. Errol C. Sull is the author of this special guide to employment. Aardvark Publishing. ISBN 0-9627558-0-x.

- Interviews

How to Turn a Technical Interview into a Winning Battle: For Computer Professionals. Vladimir Perelman wrote this guide to assist data processing professionals during interviews. VSP Management Consultants, Inc. ISBN 0-9631774-0-0.

Interviews That Get Jobs: A Step-by-Step Approach in the Job Hunt. Juanita Price is the author of this step-by-step approach. Kendall/Hunt Publishing Company. ISBN 0-8403-5550-5.

One Hundred One Great Answers to Tough Interview Questions. Ron Fry is the author. Career Press, Inc. ISBN 0-685-50637-1.

The Complete Q&A Job Interview Book. Jeffrey G. Allen is the author. Wiley, John & Sons, Inc. ISBN 0-471-60135-7.

- Resumes

Resumes that Knock 'em Dead. This book, written by Bob Adams, gives in-depth coverage of how to write resumes that really work. Bob Adams, Inc. Holbrook, MA.

Resumes for People Who Hate to Write Resumes. This fast and easy, step-by-step book was written by Jack W. Wright. Shastar Press. ISBN 0-944020-01-1.

The Complete Resume Guide. Marian Faux wrote this book which is in its third edition. Prentice Hall. ISBN 0-13-156175-8.

More Tips on Making Your Search Successful

This book's purpose has been to guide you into effectively using your personal computer in finding a job. Now Human Resources Specialist Elizabeth Smith is going to give your job search a boost by providing some tips on the following:

- Developing your personal references

- Writing form letters and response letters

- Person-to-person networking

- Preparing for interviews

- More interviewing basics

- Awkward questions and answering strategies

- The new job—how to succeed

Many of these valuable tips can be used as you work through the chapters of this book—developing your materials on your PC. The other tips are there for your personal and professional benefit.

Developing Your Personal References

Here are some tips on preparing and presenting personal references:

- When identifying personal references, a good target is 6–12 people who've known you in the work setting and will enthusiastically attest to your abilities.

- Don't put your references directly on the resume. It takes too much space and it's just not done. Use your word processor or desktop publishing software to create a separate reference sheet.

- Talk to each of the people you've selected as a reference; they should be interested in your job search plans and may be able to direct you to good job opportunities.

- Rotate names on your reference sheet; don't overburden a favored reference. Word processing makes this easy!

Writing Form Letters and Response Letters

Using a personal referral in a query letter can be a winning strategy.
See Figure B.1.

July 15, 1992

Ms. Helen Parstrum
Director of Human Resources
Ultrane Manufacturing
4747 S. W. Bowie
St. Paul, MN 32111

Dear Ms. Parstrum:

I understand that you are a personal friend of Paul Thorenson. Paul and I are former classmates in high school, and we both attended University of Texas, El Paso. Recently, he suggested that I contact you for advice and guidance.

After a challenging and rewarding career as an Operations Manager with a Dallas firm, the company had to close its doors on May 16 of this year, I have decided to relocate to St. Paul to be nearer to my family, and I am pursuing a job search in this area.

I know that it is highly unlikely that Ultrane Manufacturing would be currently searching for an Operations Manager, and I am not contacting you in that regard. However, as a Human Resources Manager in a manufacturing environment, I am hopeful that you may be able to furnish me with the names of a few good contacts who might be of assistance in my job search. I have enclosed a copy of my resume to provide you with information about my background and potential.

Ms. Parstrum, Paul speaks highly of you and feels you would be an excellent resource regarding the St. Paul job market. I appreciate your assistance and I will be calling you within a few days to schedule a time that we can meet. I will look forward to meeting with you personally.

Sincerely,

William A. Heinlein

enc.

Figure B.1

A query letter using a personal referral, word processed with Word for Windows 2.0 and featuring a Palatino font.

You need to stand out when responding to an advertised position. See Figure B.2.

Figure B.2

Response to an advertised position, word processed with WordPerfect and featuring a New Century Schoolbook font.

July 15, 1992

Mr. Henry Crindle
Placement Manager
Dardley Manufacturing
402 Cummins Circle, Room 145
Portland, OR 97811

Dear Mr. Crindle:

Your advertisement in the Sunday Edition of the *Oregonian* for a Human Relations Specialist caught my attention. This appears to be an exciting opportunity and is very much in line with my career objectives. I am confident you will find that my qualifications and experience closely match the requirements of this position.

According to the advertisement, Dardley Manufacturing is searching for a generalist who has at least five years experience in employee relations, benefits, and employee assistance. My enclosed resume will attest to my eight years of professional experience in exactly those three areas.

Your advertisement also mentions that the candidate must possess at least a Bachelor's degree in a related field. I have a Bachelor of Science in Human Resources Management, a professional certification in the field, and I have continued to upgrade my credentials by attending seminars and workshops.

If you agree that my background is a good match for your needs, I would welcome the opportunity to meet with you personally to further discuss prospects of employment with Dardley Manufacturing. I can be reached during the day on a confidential basis at my office. The number is (501)772-6666, extension 25. Thank you for your consideration, and I look forward to hearing from you.

Sincerely,

Ralph Elude

Ralph Elude

enc.

Communication studies show you can increase your chances of being hired by sending a letter following an interview, as in Figure B.3.

Figure B.3

Responding to an interview with a follow-up letter, word processed with Windows Write and featuring a Garamond font.

July 15, 1992

Dr. Gerald Martin
Doctor's Laboratories
100 W. Mesa
El Paso, TX 79924

Dear Dr. Martin:

Thank you for the courtesy shown to me during my interview on July 14. I appreciated the short tour of your new facilities and the opportunity to discuss the Billing Manager position with you. I am very interested in this opportunity.

After the interview, it occurred to me that I may not have emphasized that I frequently act as Billing Manager. The most recent experience occurred from February through May of this year. When the Billing Manager returned from her convalescence, she was very pleased with my performance. I am confident that my Medicare billing experience and recent supervisory responsibility would be a positive asset to Doctor's Laboratories.

As you consider individuals for this position, please note my assets and possibilities as a member of your team. Thank you again for the interview, and I will look forward to hearing from you in the very near future.

Sincerely,

Cynthia L. Wade

You weren't hired? Write a nice letter back, anyway, and maybe you'll be called in for another interview when a different position opens! See Figure B.4.

Figure B.4

A letter that keeps all of the doors open, word processed with Word 5.5 for DOS and featuring a Bookman font.

July 15, 1992

Ms. Marie Tobin
Director, Data Services
XYZ Company
Anytown, VT 90021

Dear Ms. Tobin:

Again, I want to thank you for the interview on July 10. I enjoyed meeting you and hearing about your organization. Yesterday, when Ms. Thompson called to inform me that another candidate had been selected, I was disappointed. When I left your office, I really felt that I had the job.

Ms. Tobin, as you may recall from our conversation, I am anxious to move up in my field. I would greatly value your feedback regarding my skills and what I might do to enhance myself. I will be calling you in a few days to see when it might be a convenient time to talk with you again.

The very best wishes to your new administrative assistant. Thank you for your assistance.

Sincerely,

Sam Martin

Sam Martin

Person to Person Networking

An intelligent job search is dependent upon intelligent networking. Besides on-line networking, there's the face-to-face kind, too. You'll want to:

- Let friends and family know of your job hunt.

- Join professional organizations and participate.

TIP

You have computer skills, so join a PC user group. Most big cities have them, and so do many smaller communities. Generally, members come from a variety of professions, and like to talk to each other!

- Research companies that interest you, and ask friends if they know anyone who works there.

- Volunteer your time to activities that are related to your career goals.

- Contact former employers, co-workers, teachers, neighbors, and mentors.

- Use special resources such as veteran's associations, Urban League, state employment counselors, or civic groups for the unemployed.

- Contact people who interviewed you but did not select you. They may be very willing to refer you to someone else.

- Check out the career placement offices at local colleges, community colleges, and your own school.

- Attend meetings, conventions, and trade shows.

- Request courtesy interviews and ask for referrals.

As you go through the process of networking, be attentive to writing thank-you notes, as appropriate. You can use database or other software to maintain a log of who you contacted, and all the pertinent information. Continuously update your list of contacts. You may want to keep a small notebook handy to jot down names and addresses that you'll enter into your database.

Networking should not be a shotgun exercise. Have a plan, and execute it. You're the best manager of your job hunt.

Preparing For Interviews

Remember the skills worksheet you filled out and the word processing files you developed before you created a resume? Review these materials before the interview. Be ready to present your accomplishments, your strengths, and your weaknesses.

You can also use cut and paste operations to assemble an interview game plan, complete with questions and answers.

Don't wait until the night before the big interview to get ready. Begin preparing the day you decide to look for a job. The simple act of sharing your plans with family, mentors, and others will assist you in organizing your thoughts. Here are some specific ideas:

1. Be prepared to discuss your strengths and weaknesses. Review the worksheets you prepared to assist in resume preparation. Pay particular attention to your accomplishments, giving thought to how you would present them to a prospective employer.

2. Look carefully at your weaknesses. Be prepared to comment. Most assuredly you will be asked about them. The best way to discuss a weakness is to point out how you have overcome the liability.

   For example,..."When I realized I had fallen behind in computer literacy, I immediately enrolled in several night classes. Then whenever a project came up that offered an opportunity to use my new skills, I volunteered. Well, soon everyone thought I was the computer genius in the office." Make sure your examples have happy endings!

Once the interview day arrives:

- Be courteous to every person you encounter.

- Remember the name of the secretary or receptionist; when you write your thank-you note, you can acknowledge them personally.

- Use your PC to acknowledge the interview in writing. Thank the company for the interview and restate how interested you are in the job.

TIP

Listen carefully to what is asked during your interview. If a question is lengthy, restate it, then answer. Use as many examples of your accomplishments as possible. Use good eye contact. Ask questions. Your homework before the interview will really pay off. Always thank the interviewer before leaving.

TIP

If you have special circumstances that require accommodations for the interview, be straightforward and let the company know when the interview is scheduled. During the interview, if you sense that a question exists as to whether you are able to physically perform the work, reassure the interviewer. Tell them how you were able to perform in your last job. Perhaps just four small blocks to elevate your desk were the only accommodations that were required.

More Interviewing Basics

Most interviewers (recruiters) are good people who are sincerely interested in conducting a good interview—one that allows the candidate to display his or her qualifications and to see if that person will "fit in" to the organization.

Recruiters have good days and bad days; too many interviews scheduled back to back makes for a bad day. While your mission is to get a second interview with the selecting official, the recruiter must make excellent referrals in order to stay in the business. Recognize this and you will find yourself in the role of helping that recruiter look good.

You can often expect to go through a series of interviews. Usually you begin with a screening interview conducted by a personnel specialist. Their job is to determine whether your qualifications meet the needs of the company. This is pretty straight forward stuff.

Be aware that you are being evaluated from the moment you respond to the invitation for the interview. That's why you should acknowledge the interview in writing. Thank them for the interview and restate how interested you are in the job.

When you arrive for your appointment be courteous to every person you encounter. When I worked for a small company as a personnel manager, I often picked up the receptionist's phone or greeted visitors when she was away from her desk. When people arrived for an interview, they threw their weight around, and demanded to see the personnel manager. You can imagine how uncomfortable they were when I would escort them to my office.

What to wear? Be conservative. Remember most employers are looking for someone who will fit in—conform. That means you will want to be in business attire. It's OK for you to wear an older suit or a dress if you are a woman. A new tie or scarf will help build your confidence. Just stay away from clothes that wrinkle, don't quite fit, or are out of style. The goal is to be comfortable, self assured, and attractive. If you are invited back for several interviews try to keep track of what you wore before, remember that each interview will be progressively more important.

A thin briefcase or folder is fine. In fact, being ready to jot down information or furnish a resume is a good practice. However, do not place your items on the interviewers desk. Keep your purse, briefcase, or folder beside you.

Listen carefully to what is asked. If a question is lengthy, restate it, then answer. Use as many examples of your accomplishments as possible when answering. Use good eye contact. Be prepared to ask the interviewer questions. Here is where doing your homework before the interview will really pay off. Always thank the interviewer before leaving.

Awkward Questions And Difficult Interviews

At best, interviewing is a lot like a blind date—two uncomfortable people, each with a different agenda, and each one with considerable risks. Employers are supposed to pose questions and make decisions based on bona fide occupational requirements. Questions regarding child care, finances, health, marital status and other questions usually are not legitimate.

But that doesn't mean these questions don't come up. How you handle the question is equally as important as the answer. If you anticipate the question coming, provide the answer before the question is posed. For example:

Interviewer: I see you live in Planeview, that's 35 miles from here. Shouldn't you be looking for a job closer to home?

Candidate: Well, there aren't many jobs in Planeview and I figure once I get employed I'll have the money to fix up my car or perhaps buy a new one.

This spells transportation problems to the interviewer—a big obstacle for the candidate to overcome. It would have been much better had the conversation gone like this:

Candidate: I'm glad you asked that question. It gives me a chance to tell you how much I enjoyed commuting in for this interview. It really doesn't take that long to drive here and I know that I will be car pooling.

The foregoing exchange allows the candidate to move on to more appropriate questions. Think of these personal-type questions as interview "housekeeping"—take care of them quickly so that you can move on to the important items.

If you are thrown an unanticipated question, answer it as best you can. If the question is clearly offensive and you are sure you don't want to work for an organization with such shoddy interviewing practices, you can say something to the effect that you fail to see the connection between the question and the job. For example:

> **Candidate**: Well Mr. Jones, I can see that we are not going to talk about the accountant position until I get through these personal questions. However, perhaps you can enlighten me regarding how my husband's job would relate to my ability to be an excellent accountant for your firm?...

The interviewer may provide an answer that shows a definite connection. So remember to keep calm and listen carefully. You have much to lose by challenging the interviewer unless the interviewer is deliberately trying to see how assertive you are. The majority of the time the questions are fairly innocent; the result of a nervous or inexperienced interviewer.

Depending on your work history, there may be very legitimate questions that must be asked and will assuredly challenge you. Say you have just been terminated, unemployed for several months, or have a history of rapid employer changes. There is no way to handle these situations but to be totally up front. Briefly explain the circumstances, do your very best to accept the responsibility of your circumstances, and add a strong statement as to how you have learned from the situation. For example:

Candidate: Yes, I was terminated from my last job. I had thought that I was ready to supervise other accountants, but I just couldn't let go. I found myself hating my job and I missed being a staff accountant. Mr. Simmons was very understanding and he will attest to my accounting skills. I know that I am a great accountant, but I lack supervisory skills.

No matter how you may have disliked Mr. Simmons or the individuals you supervised, you will not gain any points by putting down your last employer. To do so will send a strong signal that you lack loyalty and are a troublemaker.

If you are in the position of being terminated, try very hard to take it gracefully.

1. See if your supervisor is willing to give you constructive suggestions as how to handle future jobs.

2. Ask if he or she would be willing to give you a letter of recommendation.

By doing the foregoing it will be much easier to move on to the next job, not carrying over negative feelings into a new situation. Additionally, you may find the previous employer to be helpful in guiding you to another position by making referrals.

The New Job—How to Succeed

The first 90 days of your new position are really a continuation of the interviewing and testing process. Most companies refer to this as the probationary period. There are two people who really want you to do well. Naturally, you want to do well—and so does the person who hired you!

During the orientation period (usually the first week) try to spend time with your supervisor to determine his or her goals and objectives for your position. You should receive a company handbook that will acquaint you with various rules of the organization. You will want to pay particular attention to items such as your appearance, wardrobe, timeliness, attendance, and, especially, attitude.

- Attend to your duties. Make sure you understand your responsibilities completely.

- Be a note taker, and don't be afraid to ask pertinent questions.

- Do not compare your new duties with how things ran at the last place.

- Be a good listener and don't be tempted to make comments about coworkers or be drawn into office gossip.

TIP

When people are dismissed during the probationary period, it is usually because the employer perceives that they either don't fit in, have a bad attitude, or have attendance problems. Frequently, the dismissal has little to do with qualifications or skills.

During the probationary period, it's not a bad idea to keep your job search alive. You may want to delay notifying people that you have accepted employment.

Should you be successful during the probationary period, then you will want to concentrate on these attributes—they will serve you well in becoming a favored employee.

- **Be adaptable**   Let people know that you are cooperative, get along well with everyone, and can be counted on as a team player.

- **Be Versatile**   Show people that you are able to handle several different jobs. Volunteer to do tasks that allow you to develop a variety of skills. That way, if your job is eliminated, you will qualify for other functions.

- **Be willing to improve**   Don't take criticism personally, think of it as feedback. Admit your mistakes and promptly make constructive efforts to improve. Don't be stingy about complimenting others, especially the people who work for you.

- Continuously update your resume and maintain files of your accomplishments within your new job. This material becomes part of files that can be used, as new projects or jobs become available.

Resume Styles

Here are four popular styles for setting up your resume: chronological, functional, linear, and military. An example of each style appears in Chapter 7.

The Chronological Resume

This resume form is a favorite among office workers, retail and service workers, and skilled craft workers. Your experience is displayed in a narrative format, and your jobs are presented from the most recent, working back five to ten years. The chronological resume generally has the following features in this order:

- **Heading**   Should be centered with your name in bold caps. The address follows on the next two lines, and then your telephone number.

- **Objective**   This is a short description of your occupational goal. Be specific and direct.

Avoid overused phrases like ". . . where my skills may be used to mutually benefit . . ." Try to steer clear of pronouns (I, we, me), and articles (the, that, and so on).

TIP

If your job hunt is confidential, then use your home number. You can always refer to a confidential office number in your cover letter.

- **Experience**   Begin with your most recent position and work backwards.

  Five to ten years of progressive experience will produce a strong resume. Put forth your strongest and best experience, and make sure every sentence has impact.

- **Education/Training**   List the highest level of education first, using this format:

  B.S., City University, 1984
  Major: Accounting
  GPA 3.84/4.00
  Activities: President, Accounting Club

  Mention your grades only if they are above 3.00 (on a 4.00 scale). If you have recent training and no formal education, the following entry would be appropriate:

Supervisory Training, 40 Classroom Hours
Pittsburgh, PA, 1988

- **References**   It is best to leave this out of your resume but if you must have it, then this is the acceptable entry:

References available upon request.

The Functional Resume

Functional resumes are a frequent choice by people who have a difficult work history.

If you have employment gaps, are changing careers, have been underemployed, or lack formal education, you may fare better with the functional resume. This style contains the following topics:

If you have solid, progressive experience, carefully weigh the use of a functional resume. In some instances, it may trigger unnecessary doubt regarding your qualifications.

- **Heading**   Your name in full caps followed by address and home telephone number. See the comments section on Chronological Resumes.

- **Summary**   The functional resume features a summary rather than an objective, and displays the scope of your experience. For example:

"Ten years professional experience in the field of Human Resource Management." Additional sentences may be added to state your education and knowledge in your field.

- **Accomplishments**   Using your personal worksheet, organize your accomplishments by functions related to your career specialty. For example, a Human Resources Management Specialist may have functional areas such as: Recruitment, Employee Relations, and Employee Benefits.

Then, select major accomplishments that support each function. List functions and supporting accomplishments in order of strongest first. Always begin your statement with an action word.

- **Work History**   The listing of employers should begin with the most recent and work backwards.

- **Education**   This section can be titled training or education, depending on what you want to display.

- **References** Use this space for activities, military experience, or other memberships.

The Linear Resume

This resume style uses the best features of the chronological and functional resume, and is clearly the resume of the '90s.

- This style eliminates the very limiting objective statement, replacing it with a summary.

- It relies on crisp bullets to highlight experience rather than the cumbersome narrative format of the chronological resume.

- Accomplishments are added directly in the work history.

The linear resume is an excellent choice for the job hunter who has a strong work history and distinguished accomplishments. The format style is comfortable for the reader because it may use bullets and it features short, high impact statements.

This is not the format style for the job hunter who has been underemployed, has lengthy employment gaps, or lacks progressive experience. The linear resume contains the following topics, usually in this order:

- **Heading**   Your name in full caps followed by address and home telephone number. See comments under the heading section on chronological resumes.

- **Summary**   The same format is used as the functional resume. Begin with a clear statement of your length of experience, followed by strengths and special skills.

  If your length of experience is more than 20 years and you are not applying for a managerial position, you may want to say something like:

  Seasoned experience in . . .

- **Work History**   This section uses a variety of formatting styles: bold, underlining, and bullets.

  You may choose a short statement preceded by a bullet or a short narrative following the name of the company, your title, and possibly information about the company.

  The narrative may briefly state your responsibilities. Refer to your personal worksheet and select your best accomplishments. Begin with your strongest, and use percentages for greater impact.

- **Education**   Refer to the sections on education in both the functional and chronological resumes.

- **Optional**   Use this section to display memberships, publications, certifications, or military background.

The Military Resume

Because of recent defense cutbacks there are thousands of military members seeking employment. While this section is directed to service members, the information may be helpful to others.

Employers are seeking dependable, skilled workers. In addition to having specific qualifications, assets such as

- Integrity
- Physical fitness
- Leadership
- A can-do attitude

are all highly regarded. Further, the ability to be part of a team and to work successfully with a diverse work force are also highly desirable assets. Your biggest challenge is to communicate your qualifications in understandable language.

The personal worksheet will assist you in breaking down each assignment for occupational areas that relate with your experience and training. After you have completed this exercise, share this information with a career counselor or outplacement counselor. The military has excellent help available to you—all part of your benefits.

You may also visit with State Employment Counselors or Veteran's Assistant Counselors. Your goal is to translate your military skills into understandable language that adequately displays your usable skills.

Once you've identified civilian jobs that meet your service experience, the next step is to prepare your resume, contact references, and develop a network strategy. As you contact references, make sure they are fully aware of your job goals and can relate them to a potential employer.

The decision as to what resume format to choose depends on your experience. While there isn't a distinctive military style, if you have progressively responsible skills, use a linear or chronological resume. Many military members automatically lean toward a functional resume—offering very general experience. If you have specialized skills and progressive experience, you cannot market it adequately with a functional resume. On the other hand, if you have been bounced around in a variety of assignments in different levels or responsibility, you may want to use a functional resume.

TIP

No matter what resume format you decide on, perform the mother-in-law test. Show your resume to your mother-in-law (or some other person who is nonmilitary). Ask this person if they understand what you have written. If they can't, try rewording your sentences. This will ensure that a prospective employer can understand your skill and experience.

Commercial Information Services

Here is a listing of some major commercial information services to help you in your job search:

Adnet Online
5987 East 71st Street
Suite 201
Indianapolis, IN 46220
(800) 682-2901

America Online
8619 Westwood Center Drive
Vienna, VA 22182-9806
(800) 227-6364

CompuServe
5000 Arlington Center Blvd.
Columbus, OH 43220-9988
(800) 848-8199

Dialog Information Services, Inc.
3460 Hillview Ave.
Palo Alto, CA 94304
(800) 334-2564

Executive Telecom System, Inc.
9585 Valpariso Court
Indianapolis, IN 46268
(800) 421-8884

Prodigy Services Company
445 Hamilton Ave.
White Plains, NY 10601
(800) 822-6922

Public Bulletin Board Systems (BBS)

OPM
Newark, NJ
(201) 645-3887
(This is an employment BBS for federal government positions.)

JobTrac Jobs Network
Dallas, TX
(214) 349-0527
(Employment data base)

Career Connection
Aurora, CO
(303) 671-0801
(Employment data base)

Special Interest Bulletin Board Systems By Category:

Accounting

Rbase 5000
Plano, TX
(214) 881-0313

CapitalPAF UG
Layhill, MD
(301) 989-8960

SoftCopy
Tampa, FL
(813) 837-1852

Biomedical Engineering

National Biomed Engineer
Omaha, NB
(402) 559-6023

BioMed
Mather AFB, CA
(916) 362-4298

Business

Business
Altamonte, FL
(407) 682-2018

Computer Science

Illinois State University
Normal, IL
(309) 438-7370

Desktop Publishing

Desktop Publishing
Durham, NC
(919) 286-3195

Windows
Sacramento, CA
(916) 387-1264

Education

Science Line
Washington, DC
(202) 328-5853

NASA Information Technology Center
Washington, DC
(202) 453-9008

Electronics

IEEE Rochester
Rochester, NY
(716) 288-5230

IEEE Field Services
Piscataway, NJ
(908) 981-9190

Genetics

ACOG
Washington, DC
(202) 479-0005

Medical

Nurses Corner
Orlando, FL
(407) 299-4762

Law & Legal

PC Law
San Diego, CA
(619) 272-6615

Index

C

G